Beyond February

Teaching Black History
Any Day, Every Day, and
All Year Long,
K-3

President Barack Obama

Jean-Michel Basquiat

madam C.J. Walker

James Hemings

marsha P. Johnson

Georgia Gilmore

Parks

7053

Dawnavyn M. James

Routledge
Taylor & Francis Group

NEW YORK AND LONDON

A Stenhouse Book

Published in 2024 by Routledge
605 Third Avenue, New York, NY 10017
4 Park Square, Milton Park, Abingdon, Oxon OX14 4RN

Routledge is an imprint of the Taylor & Francis Group, an informa business

Library of Congress Cataloging-in-Publication Data
Names: James, Dawnavyn, author.
Title: Beyond February : teaching black history any day, every day, and all year long,
    K-3 / Dawnavyn James.
Other titles: Teaching black history any day, every day, and all year long, K-3 Description:
Portsmouth : Stenhouse Publishers, 2024. | Includes bibliographical
    references and index.
Identifiers: LCCN 2023018082 (print)
    9781625316059 (paperback)
Subjects: LCSH: African Americans—History—Study and teaching (Elementary)
Classification: LCC E184.7 .J364 2024 (print) |
    DDC 973/.0496073--dc23/eng/20230428
LC record available at https://lccn.loc.gov/2023018082

Interior design, and typesetting by Gina Poirier Design
Cover and interior illustrations by Lauren Semmer

ISBN: 9781625316059 (pbk)
ISBN: 9781032680675 (ebk)

DOI: 10.4324/9781032680675

To Matilda, Callie Will, Ira B.,
and Alberta—my foremothers.
Because of your stories,
I can tell my own.

Contents

Foreword

Not everything that is faced can be changed;
but nothing can be changed until it is faced.

—James Baldwin

Currently in the United States, the stories and histories of marginalized groups are being silenced. Baldwin's words remind us of the importance of facing the difficult truth of the past in order to make steps towards change. In *Beyond February* by Dawnavyn James, we are invited to learn and celebrate Black history in our classrooms.

In a study conducted by Janine Jones, Black middle school–aged girls participated in after-school programs that were designed to focus on community building and learning about Black culture. They were then assessed to see how they felt about themselves and their identities after participating in the program. The study revealed that after six weeks of participation in the program, "school engagement among participants increased, whereas it decreased among students in the control group" (Eckart 2017). Studies like Jones's reinforces the importance of and need for students, specifically Black students, to engage in opportunities that validate and allow for an exploration of their identities and culture.

Beyond February is an essential read for educators. It is the story of our country, and it is a story that is too often left untold. When we teach Black history, we are teaching students about the contributions of Black people to our society. We are teaching them about the struggles that Black people have faced, and we are teaching them about the resilience of the Black community. *Beyond February* encourages us to go beyond the people, the books, the curriculum, and the month of February to embrace the importance of integrating Black histories throughout the entire school year.

In this book, Dawnavyn lays out the fundamental steps that can aid educators in teaching Black history throughout the entire year. Her approach invites readers to not only engage but to go beyond. This book is a valuable resource for educators who understand the importance of teaching Black history. *Beyond February* provides a comprehensive overview of various elements of Black history, and it offers practical tips for teaching Black history in the elementary classroom.

How do we help our young learners take action? How do we help them become allies and co-conspirators? How do we help them unlearn harmful biases/stereotypes/ideas and become critical and conscious changemakers? We do that through and within our classroom and library spaces. While the work of ensuring our classroom spaces are inclusive may seem overwhelming and never-ending, it is of the utmost importance that we work to create a space where all of our students feel respected, seen, and heard. Dawnavyn sets us up to create these spaces.

—Vera Ahiyya, author of *Rebellious Read Alouds: Inviting Conversations About Diversity with Children's Books*

Acknowledgments

I grew up in a home that had a big portrait of Jesus and Martin Luther King Jr. sitting across from each other and having a conversation in heaven. My daddy recently showed me that portrait, and it's actually not as big as it looked when I was a child. I remember staring up at it and wondering what these two Black men could be talking about while sitting in heaven. There were many nights that I would wake up out of my sleep or lie wide awake with ideas for this book. I thank God for His wisdom and guidance on what to say and how to say it.

Mama, remember a couple of years ago when you told me that I should write a book and I told you that I was not going to do it? As you can see, you and God knew what was to come for me; y'all always do.

To my dad for passing down the intelligence of the Jameses. For looking over my shoulder, even when I didn't want you to, and helping me edit and revise my papers in high school. For the moments we spent editing the local newspapers and doing crossword puzzles, thank you. You, sir, are one of my favorite writers.

Max, my little brother and greatest friend, your years of encouragement, support, and protection keep me going. When no one else believed in me, you did.

Morgan, Shardae, and Lindsey, you saw my potential before I ever could. Your prayers, phone calls, FaceTimes, text messages, and conversations hold me up, and for that I am grateful.

To my godson, Sawyer, for your honesty and your participation in sharing Black histories with everyone you meet. You once told me to never give up, and because of you, my sweet boy, I didn't.

Raquel, you were there when this entire process began. Through my writer's block, questions, brainstorming rants, pages of notes, and long nights of sitting on the phone with me as I wrote, you always listened, gave your sincere opinions, and from the long distance between us, held my hand through this experience. I will never be able to thank you enough.

I can write this book because of the students and families I fell in love with during my years of teaching. To all those families, some of whom I am still in touch with, your support is unmatched. Thank you for valuing me as a teacher, coming to your children's Black history presentations, buying us books and supplies to enhance our Black history work, and giving me your feedback on how your children were sharing these Black histories with families and friends.

To the Young Historians of The Black History Club and their families, that hour we spent on Zoom was the highlight of my week! Seeing how you all created a community and how you all were able to take what we learned virtually into your classrooms and communities was the encouragement I needed to keep this work going.

To the students whose work I use in this book, thank you for your participation, your questions, your research, and for helping me show people that you're never too young to learn Black histories. Because of you, I can share with others the power of Black histories in the classroom.

To my godparents, Cassandra, Cornelius, and Kelsa, thank you for funding and sharing my work through word of mouth and on social media. Thanks for loving me through life.

To LaGarrett King, thank you for providing a space within the Teaching Black History Conference to connect with other Black history researchers and enable me to share my love and passion for elementary Black history education. *Beyond February* was born during a session I presented with Taylor, Bekah, and Brianne as we shared ways to build a Black history program.

Leo Glazé and Tasha Dhoot, thank you for your constant support and your questions, and for challenging me to expand on my thoughts and ideas throughout this process. I always looked forward to what y'all were going to say about each chapter and how I could make this book better for readers.

To Shannon, thank you for all the work you did to find the images with which I wanted to fill this book and to Dr. Lindsey E. Jones, thank you for being a fantastic fact-checker.

Kassia, thank you for always reading my mind, hearing my voice, and being the best editor ever!

To those of you who gave me space to write, speak, and teach about elementary Black history education and all its possibilities, thank you.

Introduction

When students ask teachers not to sugarcoat history, they're asking their teachers not to lie to them. There are age appropriate ways to tell the truth without lying.

—Leo Glazé (2021)

I am an enterprising hair care entrepreneur,
philanthropist, and political activist.
I invented the hot iron process for straightening hair.
I'm reported to be the first self-made woman millionaire.
Who am I?

When I was eight years old, I stood in front of a sanctuary full of people in my community. My mama, daddy, grandmother, great aunts, cousins, little brother, and other members of my church stared back at me. With a head full of ponytails, I wore a plaid dress with stockings and shoes, and I held a hair brush and a hot comb in my hands. I gave a speech describing the early life, successes, and achievements of a Black woman I had been researching for weeks (Figure I.1).

Do you know who I was? I was Sarah Breedlove, also known as Madam C. J. Walker. Born in 1867, Madam Walker was an entrepreneur and the first Black woman to be a millionaire in America. As a child, I had no idea that a woman who looked like me made the hair care products and tools my mama used on my hair every day. And ever since learning about Madam Walker as an eight-year-old, I have had this itch to find out more.

That same day, my church community also heard from Martin Luther King Jr. and Malcolm X through the voices of my dad and godfather, who each read one of their speeches. My brother, who was just four at the time, became George Washington Carver and was mostly eager to take a bite out of the home-made peanut butter and jelly sandwich at the end of his speech.

Church was that place in my community where I learned about and fell in love with Black history, and as I fell deeper in love, more and more questions began to bubble up

FIGURE I.1 Dawnavyn performing at her church's 1999 Black history program as Madam C. J. Walker.

in my mind. What else, I wondered, had Black people done throughout history? What other inventions were we responsible for? And why was what I learned at home and in my church community so different from what I learned at school? Why had I only learned about Martin Luther King Jr. at school, but both Martin Luther King Jr. *and* Malcolm X at home? The itch to find the answers to my questions only increased the older I got, as I continued to learn important and amazing things about Black people, culture, and histories.

Teaching Through Histories

Dr. LaGarrett King, the director of the Center for K–12 Black History and Racial Literacy Education at the State University of New York at Buffalo, said "History with a 'y' denotes a singular narrative, but when we think about histories, our histo*ries* have multiple perspectives. When people say you cannot teach history this way, or you cannot teach about Black history, what they are really saying is that they don't believe in our humanity, because they understand who we are through *their* history. . . . But for us to be effective citizens, we have to understand all of our citizens" (*Mills Quarterly* 2022).

As a child, I learned Black histories from my family, but very few Black histories at school. I learned history in school, yes, but it was not the same Black history I was learning at home. My family was exposing me to the innovation, pride, strength, determination, and achievements of Black people and culture. At school I was taught about the marching of Martin Luther King Jr., the tiredness of Rosa Parks, American slavery, and how Abraham Lincoln ended slavery with the Emancipation Proclamation.

Once I decided to become a teacher, I knew that I didn't want any of my students to have that same constant itch and those same unanswered questions that I had growing up. I wanted to immerse them in rich Black histories. I wanted to introduce them to Black scientists, inventors, writers, athletes, artists, and so much more. I wanted my students to ask their own questions about this country's history. And, as their teacher, I wanted to feel prepared to help my students seek out the answers to these questions, to be a learner beside them, and to make sense of history and how it has shaped the world we live in today.

That same hot comb that I held during my speech about Madam C. J. Walker has been in the hands of many of my own students. The information that I shared with my church community as a child, I have continued to tell my students each year. Those Black histories that I was exposed to at eight have seeped into my classroom through books, music, photographs, and conversations.

An Invitation

I imagine that you are holding this book in your hands because you also feel an itch. You may feel curious to explore the histories you did not learn about in school. And you likely have noticed Black histories missing from the standards and curriculum you teach. Perhaps you share my passion for teaching Black histories in ways that honor an honest telling of our country's history and celebrate Black people's contributions to it. But perhaps you are also feeling a little uncertain. If you yourself did not have a robust Black history education and your curriculum does not center Black histories, you may be asking yourself questions like "Where do I begin?" and "What if I mess up?" If you feel this way, you are not alone. One recent study of Black history education showed that while nearly 69 percent of the 217 educators in the study said they taught

Black history, only about 29 percent of them said they felt adequately prepared to do so (Figure I.2; Pitts 2020).

Our own education, our teacher education, and our life experiences did not prepare many of us to teach Black histories. Yet we must get prepared. We all, as educators, share the responsibility to teach that Black history is American history and world history. We all share the duty as educators to take the Black histories that sit and wait to be shared in February and bring them into our classrooms now and all year long.

This work of teaching and learning Black histories alongside our students may or may not be celebrated in the places we live and work. In a time in which books about Black histories are being banned from schools, and educators are fighting to ensure that standards and curricula are representative and inclusive, teaching Black history will not always be popular. But teaching Black history is both necessary and beautiful work.

So I present this invitation to you. An invitation to learn, unlearn, and engage in Black histories. An invitation to explore, research, and get uncomfortable. An invitation, regardless of what you teach, whom you teach, or where you teach, to challenge the narrative that Black histories are to be kept locked in February for Black History Month, instead of studied and celebrated in the classroom all year long.

You are cordially invited to go beyond February with me.

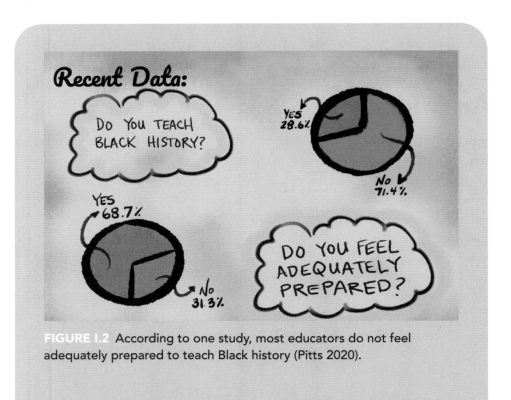

FIGURE I.2 According to one study, most educators do not feel adequately prepared to teach Black history (Pitts 2020).

Beyond the People

powerful people sets

mary fields

Augustus Jackson

Learning Black history liberates all children.

—David A. Love (2022)

"**Ms.** James! I think George Washington Carver left his peanuts here!" shouted out Percy, a five-year-old in my multiage class.

"You did say that he came to visit us today," nodded Mia.

Earlier that morning, prior to Percy's announcement to the entire class, my students had "met" George Washington Carver (Figure 1.1). They met a man they previously had no idea even existed. A man whom they were coming to know as a teacher, inventor, botanist, and scientist who created soaps, glue, paint, and other items using peanuts. In their first meeting with Carver, I introduced students to a plush representation of him, and they had the opportunity to hold him. I also passed around a bag of peanuts and a jar of peanut butter as we talked about who he was. We watched a short video on the Flocabulary website to better understand Carver's life and his contributions to science. And as my students learned about Carver, I too continued to learn about a man I thought I knew pretty well. I learned that he created a school on wheels called the Jesup Agricultural Wagon to teach farmers about crop rotation, fertilization, and other farming tools and strategies to which they otherwise might not have had access. I learned that Carver created items using sweet potatoes and soybeans as well as peanuts.

So when we found a bag of peanuts on the floor as we were lining up for recess, it was only right that we acknowledged the presence of the scientist, teacher, inventor, and botanist we met in our classroom. As my students learn about Carver and many other Black scientists, mathematicians, artists, activists, and history makers, they learn about them as whole people, as people who did extraordinary things, but also as people who are in many ways just like us. The Black historical figures we meet become my students' teachers, friends,

FIGURE 1.1 The George Washington Carter plush doll that my students "met" as we began our study of Carver's life, alongside a display of nut products

and mentors, so it only seemed natural that Percy might think that Carver had dropped by the classroom and left his peanuts behind.

Throughout this chapter, we'll think about big and small ways we can introduce (or reintroduce) our young students to Black people who made (or who are still making!) history. And although many of us received just a few crumbs of Black history education throughout our years in school, we will learn how to do better by the students in our classrooms.

A Few Essential Ideas for Teaching About Black Historical Figures

Social studies and history in the primary grades are often taught through biographies of important people. So it makes sense that we as educators think deeply about whose lives we study, what parts of their lives we focus on, and how we make connections between that one person and a broader understanding of both the past and the present.

The following sections describe some essential ideas to keep in mind as you begin to plan for teaching about Black historical figures.

Essential Idea 1
Teach About the Whole Person

When it comes to Black historical figures in the classroom, Dr. Martin Luther King Jr. is probably the most studied person. Students often learn about Dr. King in January—around his birthday and the national holiday named after him. If you walk into classrooms across the country learning about King, you're likely to see some of the same sorts of activities again and again: perhaps a teacher reading a book about King and showing a black-and-white photo of him speaking, or maybe children listening to a part of his "I Have a Dream" speech and writing about their own dreams. Students often walk away from these lessons learning that King marched and spoke for the unity of Black and white people. So, what's missing from these lessons? Students rarely learn the details or nuances of King's life. They're unlikely to learn that he was admitted to Morehouse College at the age of fifteen; that his wife, Coretta Scott King, was an activist and civil rights leader too; or that he received his PhD from Boston University in 1955. They will rarely see King as a whole person. In their book, *Social Studies for a Better World*, Noreen Naseem Rodríguez and Katy

Swalwell "encourage educators to lean into the complexity of a diversified range of significant individuals' lives by humanizing rather than heroifying them" (2022, 89). When we teach and learn the same repeated, superficial narratives about a person, we're missing the opportunity to have a robust and layered understanding of history and our current world.

A few years ago, I attended the first Teaching Black History Conference, hosted by the Center for K–12 Black History and Racial Literacy Education. During this conference I had the opportunity to attend a presentation by Dr. Amanda Vickery called "Reclaiming Our Time: Using Journey Boxes to Teach Black Women's History." Dr. Vickery shared the idea of having students collect quotes, news articles, and family and work history to transform a shoe box into a journey box that tells a more whole story of a woman in Black history, rather than solely focusing on the one thing for which they are most famous.

Shortly after learning about journey boxes from Vickery, I engaged in a similar project with students in my multiage (K–5) classroom. As my experience with journey boxes grew, however, I began to look beyond them just as physical artifacts for students to produce and more as a mindset about how we should study Black history. What if we stopped focusing on the one thing many people know about a Black historical figure or historical event and started looking at the whole picture and the whole person?

With this idea of a journey box in mind, I began doing the work of teaching the whole person with Dr. Martin Luther King Jr. As a student, I learned only a few facts about Dr. King—that was it! As I got older and became an educator, I began to learn more about the events and people that shaped King's life and saw the importance of sharing them with my students. Instead of learning about King for just one day, we can look for ways to extend that learning in small and big ways. In addition to showing black-and-white photos of King delivering his speeches, I began to show students photos of King with his family, of him as a child, of him sitting in the pulpit preparing to preach, of him on vacation, and his mug shot. Showing photos of different parts of King's life enables even the youngest of students to understand him as a nuanced, whole person, rather than as a one-dimensional hero.

In addition, in order to fully humanize and teach about individuals in history, we must understand the movements of which they were a part and the people who surrounded and worked alongside them. Instead of just reading a book about Dr. King, I also began to read my students books such as *Coretta Scott*, written by Ntozake Shange and illustrated by Kadir Nelson (which highlights the life and work of King's wife, a leader in her own right), and

Let the Children March, written by Monica Clark-Robinson and illustrated by Frank Morrison (which features King, but centers the children who marched and protested in the Children's Crusade of 1963). I showed students photos of King with other Civil Rights Movement leaders, such as Malcolm X, Roy Wilkins, Jesse Jackson, and Reverend Ralph Abernathy, to help them understand that King was one important person in a movement full of brilliant and dedicated people.

Remember earlier when I asked what was missing from the usual narrative about Dr. Martin Luther King Jr.? There is so much more to King, his fight and his leadership, than is usually presented in schools. He was a man, a father, a preacher, a friend. He was a leader and a son and a brother. He was more than a speech. He was more than a march. And he wasn't the only one doing important work during the Civil Rights Movement. As we introduce students to any Black historical figures, we should do all we can to understand and share about them in ways that illuminate their whole story and humanity.

Essential Idea 2

Expand Beyond the People Who Appear in Your Curriculum

In standards, curricula, and classrooms across the country, students tend to learn about the same Black people in history year after year. Students learn a few facts about Martin Luther King Jr., Rosa Parks, Harriet Tubman, and George Washington Carver, and then we call it a day, only to repeat the same few facts about the same few people in the next grade. Teaching in this narrow, surface-level way leads children to believe that there are only a few people worth remembering in Black history and that their contributions can be easily and neatly summed up. One bold shift that we as educators can make is to introduce our students to a diverse group of Black people in history. If we teach about Rosa Parks as a leader in the Civil Rights Movement, we can also teach about Claudette Colvin, Ruby Bridges, John Lewis, Georgia Gilmore, Aretha Franklin, Mahalia Jackson, and the children who participated in the Children's Crusade of 1963. Yes, we can hope for and work toward curricula and standards that present a more representative, truthful, and robust history of our country. But as teachers, we can also do this work right now both by teaching the people presented in our curriculum and standards in a fuller way and by going beyond those people who are most often taught in school.

Essential Idea 3
Teach the Truth

Although some repeated narratives present surface-level, but technically accurate, facts about Black people in history (e.g. "Martin Luther King Jr. gave speeches," or "Rosa Parks refused to give up her seat"), some of the most commonly repeated narratives we learned in school and may even have taught to children ourselves are partially or completely untrue.

Perhaps one of the most commonly repeated false narratives is that Rosa Parks was a tired seamstress riding home from work one day, who just decided, on a whim, that she would not give up her seat to a white passenger. As Parks herself described in her autobiography, "People always say that I didn't give up my seat because I was tired, but that isn't true. I was not tired physically, or no more tired than I usually was at the end of a working day. I was not old, although some people have an image of me as being old then. I was forty-two. No, the only tired I was, was tired of giving in" (1992, 116). In actuality, Parks was a dedicated activist long before and long after her refusal to give up her seat on the bus. (We'll keep digging more into Rosa Parks's true history later in this chapter.)

We are most afraid to tell the truth, especially to young children, when talking about the enslavement of Africans in the United States. The most dangerous thing we can do as educators is to sugarcoat the history of slavery in the United States. The most dangerous thing we can do as educators is to ignore the fact that the United States was built from the forced labor of Africans stolen from their homes and documented as property. The most dangerous thing we can do as educators is to lie to our

TEACHER TIP

It is critical that we as teachers use language that centers the humanity of people. Rather than referring to people as "slaves," we can use (and invite students to use) terms like *enslaved people*. We can also use such terms as *enslaver* (rather than *master*), *escaped* (rather than *ran away*), and *forced labor* (rather than *work*). We may not always say the exact right words, and students may be imprecise in their language, but our words do matter. When we talk about enslavement, we should always seek to center the humanity of the people who were enslaved and never shy away from choosing words that accurately represent slavery as cruel and inhumane.

students. In "An Educator's Guide to The 1619 Project: Born on the Water," Aeriale Johnson writes that "we cannot make sense of the racism that persists in the United States of America today without looking back. Without looking back, we cannot move forward" (2021, 4).

Too often we want slavery in the United States and the enslavement of Africans to be safe for our students to hear about. We want to make this history easy for them to swallow, so we tell them the bare minimum or lie about the role slavery played not just in the United States but around the world. No matter how uncomfortable it may be, we must tell the truth of how Africans were stolen from their homes. We must tell the truth of how Africans were transported to different countries on ships, stacked on top of one another. We must tell of how Africans resisted getting on or staying on ships that were carting them to unknown lands. We must tell the truth of the treatment of Africans on plantations. We must tell the truth of how families were torn apart and how children were sold to the highest bidder. We must tell the truth of the forced labor Africans and African Americans had to endure in fields. We must tell the truth of the living conditions of the enslaved. We must tell the truth of the documentation of human beings as property of other human beings.

But we must not always start there. I do my best to steer away from introducing my students to Black history through the enslavement of Africans here in the United States. It can be very dangerous to begin your teachings of Black history with the enslavement of Africans because it can often lead children to believe that Black history itself began with enslavement. It can be dangerous for children to believe that Black people come only from American slavery. Black people come from love, beauty, kingdoms, and warriors. Remember to teach your students the truth about Africa and the beauty within it. There is so much that children can learn about the many different countries on this second-largest continent. Although slavery is a part of history that we can't skip over or make more comfortable, teaching a full and true history also means that we should be teaching many diverse parts of Black history. Don't just teach the truth—teach the whole truth and nothing but the truth.

As we teach about Black history makers in our classrooms, it is important that we as teachers also do our own learning about the people we teach. And although it is important to do this research before we begin teaching about a person, we can also model that we too are continuing to learn (and unlearn) alongside our students. When exploring the role that the Black Panther Party for Self-Defense played in Black history, I had always thought and learned from society that they were a group of violent Black men and women. They wore all black and carried weapons in the streets. However, the more I learned about the Panthers, the more I learned how wrong I was. The Panthers were about community, Black community. They wanted Black people to function on their own, they wanted to end police brutality against the Black community, and they wanted to help and serve their community. I interviewed my uncle Bryan, who had some experience in the sixties with the Black Panthers in Kansas City, Missouri. He shared with me, as I later shared with some of my students, that at first, he too was afraid of the Panthers. But

he learned, with the help of his mother (my grandma), that the Black Panthers would protect him as he headed to school each day and would watch the neighborhood to protect anyone else who needed protection. So when I introduced the Black Panther Party to my students in an after-school group I run called The Black History Club, I gave them the same space I allowed myself. I gave them space to investigate the Black Panther Party for themselves and draw their own conclusions about who they were. But before I could even give them the space to investigate and make conclusions, I had to do the work first. I had to be sure that I was giving my students truthful information and being intentional about not sharing a narrow or false narrative. I gathered resources, and together with my students, we studied photographs, songs, and books. And while there is not nearly enough information written for children about the Black Panther Party, we did collect some important information from *Civil Rights Then and Now*, written by Kristina Brooke Daniele and illustrated by Lindsey Bailey.

We also found a bit of information in the book *We the People: The United States Constitution Explored and Explained* by Aura Lewis and Evan Sargent. So what did my students conclude about the Black Panther Party? They learned that the Black Panthers ran a free breakfast program and provided food for the community (Figure 1.2). My students learned that the Black Panthers sponsored legal aid and health care clinics in Black communities. They concluded that the government saw the Panthers as a Black military. And they concluded that the goal of the Black Panthers was to protect, educate, and defend their people and communities, images of which you rarely see in popular media or in classrooms.

An episode of the PBS digital history show *Origins of Everything* titled "Is the Rosa Parks Story True?" asserts that "clearly telling historical narratives with greater detail and accuracy can inspire us all to greater action" (2018). We should strive to live by this statement in all of our teaching, but especially when teaching Black history, where so much truth has yet to be taught in schools. Let's keep learning about the truth ourselves so that we are equipped to refresh the repeated narratives with truth.

So where do we start? In the following charts you'll find a framework I use for my own learning as I prepare to teach my students about various historical figures. And while an exhaustive history of each important person could never fit in a chart, this framework does help me begin to question and push beyond repeated narratives.

FIGURE 1.2. My students and I studied historical photos of the members of the Black Panther Party serving the community, including this one in which a Black Panther member serves food to children as part of the free breakfast program.

TEACHING ABOVE AND BEYOND THE REPEATED NARRATIVE

Frequently studied person in Black history

Rosa Parks (1913–2005)

Repeated superficial or false narrative

Rosa Parks was tired after work and refused to give up her seat on the bus to a white person.

Add to a fuller, more truthful narrative.

* On December 1, 1955, Rosa Parks, a seamstress, activist, and secretary of the Montgomery, Alabama, chapter of the NAACP, refused a bus driver's order to give up her seat in the "colored section" of a bus once the "white section" was full. She was arrested for this act of civil disobedience.

* Parks played a critical role in organizing the Montgomery Bus Boycott. Many other people also organized and participated in this boycott, which began on December 5, 1955, and ended on December 20, 1956. It is important to teach more broadly about the atmosphere in Montgomery, Alabama, during the Civil Rights Movement and what the bus boycott there accomplished.

* It is also important to contextualize the Montgomery Bus Boycott within the longer Black struggle for equal rights in public transportation (e.g. the *Plessy v. Ferguson* US Supreme Court decision in 1896).

* Just prior to her refusal to give up her seat on the bus, Rosa Parks attended a rally for Emmett Till that was led by Dr. Martin Luther King Jr. Till's murder pushed her to act. "I thought of Emmett Till and I just couldn't go back" (Bennett 2020).

* Fifteen-year-old Claudette Colvin, not Rosa Parks, was the first Black woman to be arrested for her refusal to give up her seat on the bus, on March 2, 1955.

* Parks was married to Raymond Parks, a barber, who was also an activist.

* Parks spent her life as a freedom fighter, working for equal rights, voting rights, and justice for the falsely accused.

Keep learning (and unlearning) and sharing with your students

In this photo, Rosa Parks is fingerprinted after her arrest in February 1956.

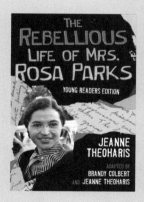

Although this biography of Rosa Parks is written for young people ages twelve and up, it's also a tremendously helpful resource for teachers.

The eight-minute video "Is the Rosa Parks Story True?" blasts myths about Parks and gives a truer, fuller picture of her as a person and activist.

Rosa, a picture book written by Nikki Giovanni and illustrated by Bryan Collier, offers students a broader and richer history of Parks than what is usually presented in schools.

TEACHING ABOVE AND BEYOND THE REPEATED NARRATIVE

Frequently studied person in Black history

Harriet Tubman (b. 1820 or 1821, died 1913). It is important to note that although scholars place Tubman's birth year as 1820 or 1821, many individuals born into slavery had no definitive way of knowing their exact birth date.

Repeated superficial or false narrative

Harriet Tubman helped free enslaved Africans and African Americans through the Underground Railroad.

Add to a fuller, more truthful narrative.

* Harriet Tubman was born in 1820 or 1821. Her parents named her Araminta Ross.

* Tubman was enslaved not in the deep South, as some assume, but in Maryland (Dorchester County).

* She sought freedom in Philadelphia in 1849 at about twenty-nine years old.

* Harriet Tubman was a key figure on the Underground Railroad, returning to the South thirteen times to help guide those who were enslaved north to freedom.

* Canada was a destination for many on the Underground Railroad, and Tubman owned a home in Ontario, Canada.

* Harriet Tubman participated in the Civil War as a soldier, spy, and nurse.

* She was an activist during the women's suffrage movement.

Keep learning (and unlearning) and sharing with your students

A portrait of Harriet Tubman

Moses, written by Carole Boston Weatherford and illustrated by Kadir Nelson, centers Tubman's faith, persistence, and bravery as she escapes enslavement and travels back south to help other African Americans make their journey to freedom.

This excellent teaching guide for *Moses* written by Tracie Vaughn Zimmer shares ways to use this book in the classroom.

TEACHING ABOVE AND BEYOND THE REPEATED NARRATIVE

Frequently studied person in Black history

George Washington Carver (born c. 1861–1864, died 1943). Carver's exact birth year is particularly difficult to determine as a result of his being born into the chaos of the Civil War in southern Missouri.

Repeated superficial or false narrative

George Washington Carver invented peanut butter.

Add to a fuller, more truthful narrative.

* Carver was a scientist, teacher, and inventor who created a traveling school on wheels to teach farmers about tools and farming methods to which they otherwise would not have had access.

* He was the first Black graduate (bachelor's in 1894 and master's in 1896) and instructor at Iowa State University. Later, beginning in 1896, he did his research and teaching at a new institution for the education of African Americans, Tuskegee Normal and Industrial Institute in Alabama (Vella 2015).

* Carver created more than three hundred different products and uses for the peanut, including soaps, cheese, paint, and glue.

* George Washington Carver was interested in peanuts because, whereas the cotton crops most commonly grown in the South depleted the soil of its nutrients over time, crops such as peanuts replenished nutrients in the soil and led to healthier farming conditions.

* As he did with peanuts, Carver also found inventive uses for the sweet potato.

Keep learning (and unlearning) and sharing with your students

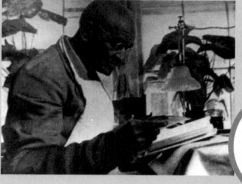

This short and informative video includes documentary footage of Carver's work and life.

The Secret Garden of George Washington Carver, written by Gene Barretta and illustrated by Frank Morrison, is a beautiful picture book that tells the story of Carver's life "from a baby born into slavery to a celebrated botanist, scientist, and inventor" (2020, front matter).

This video from Flocabulary shares information about Carver's life through music.

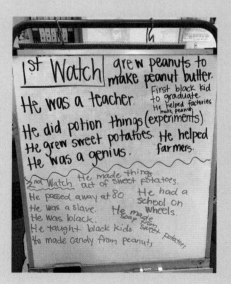

After watching the Flocabulary video about Carver, my students brainstormed this list about what they learned.

TEACHING ABOVE AND BEYOND THE REPEATED NARRATIVE

Frequently studied person in Black history

Martin Luther King Jr. (1929–1968)

Repeated superficial or false narrative

Martin Luther King Jr. was a civil rights movement leader who gave the "I Have a Dream" speech and wanted to end segregation.

Add to a fuller, more truthful narrative.

* King attended Morehouse College, where both his father and grandfather also attended.

* He went to jail several times for marching and fighting for equal rights.

* King led the Southern Christian Leadership Conference (SCLC) from 1957 until his assassination in 1968. The SCLC pioneered the strategy of nonviolent mass action—the iconic, large-scale, peaceful marches and other demonstrations. It was in his capacity as a pastor and the leader of the Montgomery Improvement Association (MIA) and the SCLC that King went to jail (Garrow 2015).

* King was married to Coretta Scott King and had four children. Coretta Scott King was also an activist and leader in the civil rights movement.

* King met Malcolm X once at a Senate hearing on Capitol Hill. The hearing was about ending segregation in public places.

* He was a preacher (also known as Reverend Dr. Martin Luther King Jr.).

Keep learning (and unlearning) and sharing with your students

King was arrested many times for acts of civil disobedience. In this photo, taken in 1958 in Montgomery, Alabama, he has been arrested for "loitering" after attempting to go to the arraignment of a man accused of assaulting his friend and fellow civil rights leader Reverend Ralph David Abernathy.

I show my students mug shots and photos of civil rights leaders getting arrested to help them understand the lengths to which police went to silence Black people for protesting even when they were protesting peacefully or in silence.

We also talk about how it was against the law for Black people to be in spaces designated only for white people, and about how people fought to change these laws. The famous black-and-white image of photographer Cecil J. Williams drinking from the "whites only" water fountain is one example of resistance that I show students.

These photos enable my students to see the power of resistance (which is often ignored in our elementary curriculum). King and many other civil rights activists were aware of what could happen to them when they took action against injustice and were prepared for it; they did it anyway because they wanted change.

This episode of the *Teaching Hard History* podcast is an excellent resource for teachers who want to learn more and better about King than we ourselves learned in school.

Although there are many children's books all about King, picture books such as *Pies from Nowhere* and *Let the Children March* feature King but highlight *other* leaders of the Civil Rights Movement who worked alongside King. These books help children understand a movement that involved many people, *and* enable them to see King in different roles than those in which he is usually shown.

In addition to viewing photos of King as an adult with his family, seeing images of historical figures like King as children helps young people understand that they too can be powerful people.

Essential Idea 4

Teach About Living People as History Makers Too

Although it is perhaps convenient to describe history as "what happened long ago" and consider it separate from our current times, part of our job as teachers is to help students make connections between what happened in the past and what is happening in today's world. As one of my young students once asked, "Why are we learning about dead Black people?" Even, and perhaps especially, with young students, it is important to balance "long ago" history with more recent history and current events. When I teach about the poet Langston Hughes, I also teach about living poet and children's book author Kwame Alexander. When I teach about Rosa Parks, I also teach about Claudette Colvin (who is still alive today!). When I teach about groundbreaking tennis players Althea Gibson and Arthur Ashe, I also teach about Venus and Serena Williams. As we teach about Black historical figures who may no longer be living, we can connect them to living people who continue to make history.

Essential Idea 5

Trust the Children in Our Classrooms

Some people argue that history must be simplified in order for young children to understand it, but I disagree. As a kindergarten teacher I have heard my students retell the events of the Tulsa Race Massacre, and I have watched them process the image of Black children in Birmingham being sprayed with fire hoses. I have watched them connect protests and marches of the past to protests and marches of today. Children are natural historians. They are curious about the world and unafraid of nuance. And while we don't expect children to learn everything there is to know about history in their first years of school, we need to trust that, from the earliest ages, they can engage in inquiry about how the world was, is, and can be in the future.

Three Ways to Weave a Study of Black Historical Figures Throughout Your Curriculum

Integrating Black histories into the curriculum you already teach can be done in bigger and smaller ways. What's most important is recognizing that there is room for Black histories in your lesson plans every day.

Make Black History Part of Classroom Life Every Day

TIMELINE: Every day in many ways

Why Make Space for This Work?

One way to push back against the idea that Black history should exist and be celebrated only during the twenty-eight days of February is to celebrate and learn Black history each and every day. We can do this in small but powerful ways when we help students make connections between what they are learning in the curriculum and Black people who have contributed to these areas of study.

A Peek into My Classroom

Mathematician of the Day

In my classroom, one way we do this work daily is through our Mathematician of the Day routine. We begin this routine at the start of the school year by highlighting a different student in our class each day as the Mathematician of the Day. Students have the chance to see themselves as mathematicians, have their work celebrated, and, in general, get excited about math.

Once each of my students has the chance to be the Mathematician of the Day, we begin to focus on mathematicians outside our classroom, including Black mathematicians, and inventors who used mathematics. At the beginning of our math class each day, my students do a drum roll as I reveal an image of our Mathematician of the Day. Along with the image, I share some facts and a story or a short video clip about the highlighted person.

One day I shared an image of Jerry Lawson, who invented the first home video game system with interchangeable games. Many of my students have handheld or game consoles at home and were excited to make the connection between math and video games and to share about the games they love to play.

Another day I shared about John Urschel, a mathematician and former football player. I showed my students photos of Urschel in his football gear, and we watched a video of him talking about his love for math. My students were thrilled to share their connections about loving both math *and* sports.

"Ms. James!!! I'm an athlete and mathematician like him!"

"Me too! I play soccer, and I'm a mathematician."

"I'm a mathematician too, but I do gymnastics."

My students were very excited that they could relate to and be like our Mathematician of the Day even though the person wasn't someone in our classroom or someone they knew. And how cool for students to see that they can be an athlete and a mathematician.

As Mathematician of the Day becomes a well-loved routine in our classroom, students begin to anticipate and look forward to it. I often hear my students excitedly ask one another, "Who's our Mathematician of the Day today?"

What Will You Try?

What Black histories are you curious about? Find people in Black history who intersect with your curricular focuses. Ask yourself what living and historical Black people have contributed to the ideas you are studying, and highlight them in small but meaningful ways that add up over time.

Integrate Mini-Studies into Your Curriculum

TIMELINE: A few days or a week for each mini-study

Why Make Space for This Work?

While some daily routines last just a few moments, integrating mini-studies into your curriculum that span a few days or a week can give students time to deeply explore an individual or topic.

A Peek into My Classroom

A Poetry Mini-Study

In my classroom, connecting students to writers, illustrators, artists, journalists, and poets is always a goal of literacy instruction. In April as part of our celebration of National Poetry Month, I introduce students to Black poets such as Maya Angelou, Useni Eugene Perkins, Carole Boston Weatherford, Walter and Christopher Myers, Mahogany L. Browne, Elizabeth Acevedo, and Kwame Alexander. We read the picture book version of Maya Angelou's poem *Life Doesn't Frighten Me* and study the illustrations by Jean-Michel Basquiat. As we read the picture book, we create movements to go along with some of the lines of the poem to help us remember the words and dig into the meaning behind those words. I also share photos of Basquiat, and we take a look at some of his artwork. Using a directed drawing activity from our favorite virtual art teacher, Ms. Haynes, students have a chance to imitate Basquiat's craft, learning more about Basquiat and the symbolism he uses in his art.

Ms. Haynes's directed drawing activity related to Jean-Michel Basquiat

More Picture Books for Studying Black Poets

Woke: A Young Poet's Call to Justice, written by Mahogany L. Browne with Elizabeth Acevedo and Olivia Gatwood, illustrated by Theodore Taylor III

Out of Wonder, written by Kwame Alexander with Chris Colderley and Marjory Wentworth, illustrated by Ekua Holmes

Hey Black Child, written by Useni Eugene Perkins, illustrated by Bryan Collier

Using Kwame Alexander's *Out of Wonder*, an anthology of "poems celebrating poets," my second graders studied the poem "Walter, Age Ten," which celebrates poet Walter Dean Myers (Figure 1.3). I enlarged a stanza of this particular poem by writing it out on a sheet of chart paper so that we could analyze and dissect it as a class. During our poetry study, we learned different strategies for finding meaning in poems, including "reading between the lines." To do this work, we read poems more than once to discover information we may not have picked up on the first time we heard or read the poem. As we read through "Walter, Age Ten," we highlighted words that were unfamiliar to us (e.g. double dutch, daddy-o, Harlem, and sweeties), and I pulled those words out of the

FIGURE 1.3. A display from a second-grade poetry mini-study

poem, writing them on sentence strips. I also found pictures that my students could associate with the unfamiliar words. I even found a photo of Myers himself at age ten! We also paired our study of this poem with Myers's book *Harlem* and the book *Love That Dog* by Sharon Creech that features poetry by Myers. The pairing of different texts, words, and photographs gave my students a fuller understanding of Myers and also enabled them to see how important his poetry was to other poets and writers.

Along with *Out of Wonder*, I had a whole shelf of books and poems written by Kwame Alexander that my students could access throughout our poetry study. As we read poems by Alexander and watched a few videos of him reciting his poems, my students got a feel for the rhythm that poetry produces.

A Math Mini-Study

"Today we are going to learn about ancient art from a country called Egypt," I announced as my kindergarten and first-grade students gathered on the carpet one morning.

"Where is Egypt, Ms. James?" asked Jake.

I grabbed a globe sitting near our meeting area and pointed. "Egypt is right here."

"That's Africa!" said Trent, excitedly.

"How did you know that?" I encouraged.

"Remember when we learned about Africa, Ms. James? There's kings and gold there!" reminds Marcus.

Using a lesson from the Institute for Arts Integration and STEAM, I integrated a mini-study of art and Black history into a two-day math lesson on comparing lengths of objects using nonstandard units of measurement. Throughout this lesson, we learned about different symbols in Ancient Egyptian art. For this particular study, we studied the sizes of different figures in the art. For Ancient Egyptians, how people were represented in their art had a special meaning. The taller a figure was, the more important they were. We looked at different pieces of Ancient Egyptian art and discussed which figures were most important and why.

After analyzing different art, students used cubes to measure and compare the heights of various figures in Egyptian art. This lesson enabled my students to see math in a different way while also applying reasoning skills and learning some African history. Because I wanted them to truly see the imagery and symbolism in the Ancient Egyptian art pieces, I decided to do a two-day lesson in which they analyzed and examined the art on day one and learned a little bit about Egypt and where it is. We then applied what they studied from the art into the math activity on the second day of the mini-study.

Integrating a study of Egyptian art into our math learning taught students that there are valuable and rich histories throughout the world that are fascinating and worthy of our study.

What Will You Try?

Whether it is written directly in our curriculum or not, Black history intersects with just about everything we teach. Perhaps you start with your own favorite content area or unit and begin to get curious. Or maybe you start with a topic about which your class is passionate. Ask yourself how Black history connects with your upcoming science focus or nonfiction reading unit. Begin by doing some research and learning yourself and think about how you can share your learning with students.

Build Dynamic Units That Center Black History

TIMELINE: A unit of study that spans a week to several weeks

Why Make Space for This Work?

While much of our teaching and learning of Black history can take place during everyday moments woven throughout our curriculum, building and reimagining units of study that are grounded in Black history is an opportunity we do not want to pass up.

Like those in many states, the social studies standards in my state ask students to study various historical figures in each grade level, describing the importance of the people and their contributions, as well as the meaning of national holidays connected to these people. Rather than only highlighting the listed historical figures in my grade-level standards (George Washington, Abraham Lincoln, Martin Luther King Jr., Squanto, and Christopher Columbus), I chose to broaden and deepen students' understanding of history and the people who make it. Black history is a critical part of American history, and it is our responsibility to teach it fully and truthfully.

A Peek into My Classroom

American History Makers

One focus of our social studies standards in my state (and many others) is identifying contributions of American history makers while also comparing the past and the present. As part of our work with these social studies standards, my kindergarten students and I engage in our own research project to discover historical people "missing" from the curriculum. We use the History Makers section of the PebbleGo website to learn about a diverse group of people and their contributions to our country and the world.

We start the project by defining, as a class, who a historical figure is and then learning a few of the ins and outs of navigating the History Makers section of the PebbleGo website. Students spend time exploring this section of the website before choosing three people who stand out to them and finally narrowing it down to one History Maker on whom to focus. Students gather three facts about their chosen History Maker and create a video to share as part of a news broadcast about important people in history.

When I introduced History Makers, I clicked on the tab that featured African Americans, and my students recognized quite a few people whom we had already "met" in our classroom. They did not have to choose African American History Makers, but it was an option many were excited to take!

What Will You Try?

Look for opportunities to center Black history throughout the content areas, units, and standards you teach. There are always ways to do this work!

It is important to remember that we can use these three ways of weaving Black history into the curriculum simultaneously. You might be learning about a Black Mathematician of the Day during one part of your day, while also doing a mini-study of Kadir Nelson's illustrations during writing time, while also connecting your study of living and nonliving things to George Washington Carver during science time. There are big and small ways of letting Black history shine every day, throughout the school year. It can be done—that's the whole idea, really.

Tools and Resources for Teaching Black History

I refer to my favorite book collections, primary sources, websites, and resources as my Black History Toolbox. This toolbox helps me explore ideas and supports me in teaching Black histories. As you read this section, consider what new tools you might add to your Black History Toolbox and how they will support you in the classroom.

Use Photos to Tell a Story

Photographs of historical events and people are some of my go-to resources for teaching. One day in my class, we were analyzing some historical photos of Martin Luther King Jr. and his life. I asked my students, "What do you see? What do you think? What do you want to know?" as we looked at each black-and-white photo.

One of my inquisitive students raised his hand and asked, "Did they see in black and white?" At first I wasn't quite sure what this kindergartener meant, so I asked him to say more.

"You know, like when people saw things. When they opened their eyes. They saw stuff in black and white?" I smiled and responded by explaining that camera film in the past could only be developed in black and white, but that later, film was designed to make color photos.

In that short conversation, I realized that for my young students, black-and-white photographs meant "old" or "long ago"—in other words, very distant from their current lives. By contrast, I've noticed that when I balance black-and-white photos with color or colorized photos, history feels more real, more connected to them. When students see historical photos in color, they often realize that some of the people and events they are learning about weren't from so long ago. History is there, in living color, for them to analyze, question, and explore.

The Library of Congress website (www.loc.gov) has an excellent searchable collection of high-quality historical photographs. And, of course, many photographs can be found by a simple Google search. When gathering a collection of older photos, consider also adding "in color" to your Google searches to find older black-and-white photographs that have been colorized.

Read Picture Books in Purposeful Ways

Although we most often think of picture books as children's books, we adults can also learn a lot about Black history through picture books. Most of us did not receive a robust education in Black history in school, so we will be working alongside our students to learn more about the people we are teaching. Many picture book biographies include information or endnotes at the back of the book that give additional background information and resources on the book's topic.

For example, after reading *Unspeakable: The Tulsa Race Massacre* by Carole Boston Weatherford or *Let the Children March* by Monica Clark-Robinson, my students always ask, "Did this really happen?" or "Was this real?" I use the author and illustrator notes in picture books not just to educate myself but also to highlight important details for my students. In these two books in particular, there are real photos at the back of the book of what happened during the events depicted in the stories. Sometimes I display these photos on the board to discuss before we read. We may analyze the pictures and discuss what we see or talk about what we think is happening. After reading the book, we go back to what we said about the photos to add to or change our initial thoughts. These extra resources are in these books for a reason—to help further our own research and spark inquiry. These resources also help answer some of the questions your students may have during the read-aloud. Let them explore books to their full capacity.

Integrate Art into Your Teaching

What I like about art is that it comes in so many different forms and that you can use those different forms to enrich and support your teaching, especially when it comes to highlighting Black histories. A few years ago, I taught first grade during summer school, and our focus for math was geometry. I decided to make the connection to architecture and have students explore the intersection between this art form and our geometry. Students were given drafting books, and each day I introduced them to a Black architect using the book *Black Built: History and Architecture in the Black Community* by Paul Wellington (2019). Each week of summer school, students designed and constructed their own structures through sculpture, painting, photography, and drawings (Figure 1.4). Some of the architects we studied had websites

FIGURE 1.4 Students learned about architecture and how architects use shapes to construct buildings.

that enabled us to interact with 3-D models of their designs and learn about their design process.

Share Hands-on Materials

I encourage you to use the tools and resources I've mentioned, but also to continually seek out new materials that will be engaging and meaningful to your students. For example, I have found dolls to be great tools to bring in and let students explore. I have often brought to class the American Girl Doll named Addy and shared her story. As illustrated earlier, a George Washington Carver doll comes to visit us each year. And I recently purchased a Maya Angelou doll and was given an Ida B. Wells doll. When we learned about Alfred L. Cralle, who invented the ice cream scoop, I brought in an actual ice cream scoop for students to explore. And, of course, food is also a fantastic tool! When we learned about potato chip inventor George Crum, we read a book about his life, did a chip taste test to see which chip was the best, and graphed our results during math class. Students always remember and continue to talk about the lessons in which we explore tools and artifacts together.

An Introduction to the Powerful People Sets

As we've discussed in this chapter, children often learn about the same Black historical figures throughout their education. And although those individuals are important, there is more to Black history than Martin Luther King Jr., Ruby Bridges, Harriet Tubman, Rosa Parks, and George Washington Carver. There are other people who stood alongside, came before, and came after them.

Each of the Powerful People Sets in the following pages helps connect you to a group of people who are important to a particular area of Black history and culture. And as much as I wanted to create a set for every big idea in Black history, that would be impossible! Instead I share with you a few sets that have engaged and educated my students. I've also included a blank template to help guide you in creating your own Powerful People Sets to bring into your classroom. (This template is also in the appendix.)

In the past, and currently, Black people have been and are creative. I hope you can use these Powerful People Sets to explore more of who Black people are and their contributions to arts, music, science, math, culinary, sports, activism, and education.

Powerful People Set 1

OUR BLACK HISTORY: Inventors and Food

BIG IDEA: We can celebrate and learn about Black people's contributions as mathematicians, scientists, and inventors throughout history and in present times.

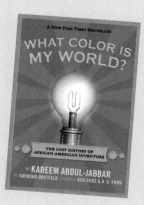

When it comes to Black history and science, students are often only introduced to George Washington Carver and his work with peanuts. But, of course, Carver isn't the only Black scientist or inventor in history. Here are three food-focused inventors who contributed greatly to what we eat today and whom you can introduce alongside George Washington Carver.

PERSON 1

George "Crum" Speck (1824–1914)

Invention: Potato chips

Did You Know? Crum ran a restaurant in Saratoga County, New York, in the 1850s. And although he is widely credited with the invention of the potato chip, it may have been his sister, Kate, who was the actual inventor (White 2017).

For More Info: Read *Mr. Crum's Potato Predicament* by Anne Renaud, *Have You Thanked an Inventor Today?* by Patrice McLaurin, and *What Color Is My World? The Lost History of African-American Inventors*, written by Kareem Abdul-Jabbar with Raymond Obstfeld and illustrated by Ben Boos and A. G. Ford. (I recommend the picture book, but there is also a chapter book version.)

Try This: Hold a potato chip tasting. Have your students try different potato chips, using their five senses. Once students have tried all the chips, have each student vote for their favorite chip and create a class graph.

PERSON 2

Augustus Jackson
(1808–1852)

Invention: A way to make ice cream last longer

Did You Know? Because of his innovative system for making ice cream and keeping it frozen, Augustus Jackson was able to supply ice cream to different shops throughout Philadelphia.

For More Info: Read *Ice Cream Man: How Augustus Jackson Made a Sweet Treat Better*, written by Glenda Armand and Kim Freeman and illustrated by Keith Mallett. This picture book offers a variety of ways to bring science, economics, and literacy into the classroom.

Try This: After listening to the song "Augustus Jackson" by Ellis Paul (from his book *The Hero in You*), write down facts students heard in the song. Then have students create a paper ice cream cone with three scoops of different ice cream flavors. On each scoop, have your students write a fact about Augustus Jackson. This would also be a great time to introduce your students to Alfred Cralle, inventor of the ice cream scoop!

"Augustus Jackson" song by Ellis Paul

PERSON 3

James Hemings
(1765–1801)

Invention: Hemings popularized macaroni and cheese in the United States, a dish that still holds great importance in African American cuisine.

Did You Know? At age nine, James Hemings; his mother, Elizabeth Hemings; and his siblings were brought to Monticello when Thomas Jefferson inherited many enslaved people from the estate of John Wayles, the father of Jefferson's wife, Martha. James Hemings was the son of Elizabeth Hemings and John Wayles, making James Hemings and Martha Jefferson half-siblings. In 1874, at the age of nineteen, Hemings traveled to Paris with Thomas Jefferson, where he learned cooking techniques from French chefs.

For More Info: Watch a clip from the Netflix show *High on the Hog*, which explains some of James Hemings's history with macaroni and cheese. Read *Jubilee: Recipes from Two Centuries of African American Cooking* by Toni Tipton-Martin (2019). (Although this is a cookbook designed for adults, I showed photos from this book to students and read them parts from the section on macaroni and cheese.)

Try This: After watching the clip about James Hemings from *High on the Hog* with your students, share a recipe for macaroni and cheese with them and have them share it with their families; you could even try making macaroni and cheese at school! Don't forget to share other varieties of macaroni and cheese recipes, such as macaroni and cheese waffles or balls!

The James Hemings clip from *High on the Hog*

Powerful People Set 2

OUR BLACK HISTORY: Activism

BIG IDEA: We can learn about the role Black women played as leaders of the Civil Rights Movement and beyond.

We often teach students about Martin Luther King Jr. and Rosa Parks and their contributions to the Civil Rights Movement. Although King and Parks *did* play critical roles in the Civil Rights Movement, they were not alone in this fight for justice and equality. This Powerful People Set highlights women who contributed to the Civil Rights Movement and women whose activism went beyond the years of the Civil Rights Movement.

PERSON 1

Ella Josephine Baker (1903–1986)

Role: Civil and human rights activist

Did You Know? Baker was a member of the NAACP and the SCLC, and was the architect of the Student Nonviolent Coordinating Committee (SNCC). She worked alongside civil rights leaders W.E.B. Du Bois, Thurgood Marshall, Stokely Carmichael, Rosa Parks, Fannie Lou Hamer, and Martin Luther King Jr.

For More Info: Read *Lift as You Climb: The Story of Ella Baker*, written by Patricia Hruby Powell and illustrated by R. Gregory Christie.

Try This: A repeated question throughout the picture book *Lift as You Climb* is "What do you hope to accomplish?" After reading the book and learning more information about Ella Baker and her work, have your students write their answers to the question, "What do you hope to accomplish?"

PERSON 2

Georgia Gilmore (1920–1990)

Role: Cook and fundraiser

Did You Know? To raise money for people to pay for gas and buy cars during the bus boycott in Montgomery, Gilmore and her group, Club from Nowhere, baked and sold pies.

For More Info: Read *Pies from Nowhere: How Georgia Gilmore Sustained the Montgomery Bus Boycott*, written by Dee Romito and illustrated by Laura Freeman. Listen to an interview with Georgia Gilmore.

Try This: Georgia Gilmore's recipe for pound cake is featured at the back of *Pies from Nowhere*. Share that recipe with your students to make at home, or bake it at school as a class. Georgia and her group also made different kinds of pies to raise money. Before reading, ask your students to see whether they can find all the flavors of pie they made listed on one of the pages of the book.

An interview with
Georgia Gilmore

PERSON 3

Claudette Colvin
(b. 1939)

Role: Civil rights activist and nurse's aide

Did You Know? At age fifteen, on March 2, 1955, Claudette Colvin was arrested for refusing to give up her seat to a white woman on the bus in Montgomery, Alabama, nine months before Rosa Parks refused to give up her seat. Colvin was also part of the federal class action suit *Browder v. Gayle* (1956), which resulted in bus desegregation in Montgomery.

For More Info: Read *Claudette Colvin: Twice Toward Justice* by Phillip Hoose. Listen to the *Podcast Radio Diaries* episode "Claudette Colvin: Making Trouble Then and Now." (It's a great listen for teachers and students alike!).

Try This: Gather resources about both Claudette Colvin and Rosa Parks and create a Venn diagram comparing their lives and activism.

The Claudette Colvin Radio Diaries podcast episode

PERSON 4

Marsha "Pay It No Mind" Johnson (1945–1992)

Role: Gay and transgender rights activist and advocate for homeless LGBTQIA youth

Did You Know? Marsha P. Johnson played a pivotal role in the Stonewall Rebellion of 1969 and was a lifelong advocate for transgender youth. Despite the challenges in her own life, Johnson was known for her generosity and creating safe spaces for transgender youth, including Sylvia Rivera. There is a bust of Marsha P. Johnson in Christopher Park in New York City.

For More Info: Read *Sylvia and Marsha Start a Revolution!*, written by Joy Michael Ellison and illustrated by Teshika Silver.

Try This: Have students research how Marsha's activism continues today and brainstorm ways in which they can advocate for and support youth in their community.

Powerful People Set 3

OUR BLACK HISTORY: The American West

BIG IDEA: We can learn about Black cowboys' contributions to the American West and the culture of cowboys.

Cowboys are such a fascinating group of people. As a child, I never saw images of Black cowboys in books or on television. Yet despite what we see in popular media, there is a rich history of Black cowboys, cowgirls, and rodeo stars. African Americans contributed a lot to the American Wild West (one in four cowboys was Black!), and that should be honored and recognized (Nodjimbadem 2017).

PERSON 1

Bill Pickett (1870–1932)

Nickname: The Dusky Demon

Job: Cowboy, rodeo star, and actor

Did You Know? Bill Pickett invented bull-dogging, a rodeo move in which the rider jumps off their horse onto a bull, grabs it by its horns, twists its head, bites its ear or lip, and wrestles it to the ground.

For More Info: Check out movie posters featuring Pickett. Read *Bill Pickett: Rodeo-Ridin' Cowboy*, written by Andrea D. Pinkney and illustrated by Brian Pinkney, and *The True West*, written by Mifflin Lowe and illustrated by William Luong.

Try This: Have your students explore BillPickettRodeo.com to see photos of bulldogging and see how Bill Pickett's legacy is being carried on by Black cowboys and cowgirls today. Have students write about how Pickett has influenced rodeo stunts and performances.

PERSON 2

George Fletcher (1890–1973)

Nickname: People's Champion

Job: Cowboy

Did You Know? George Fletcher was not always allowed to enter larger rodeos because he was Black. He was inducted into the Rodeo Hall of Fame in 2001.

For More Info: Read *Let 'Er Buck!*, written by Vaunda Micheaux Nelson and illustrated by Gordon C. James. Read more about George on the National Cowboy Museum website.

George Fletcher at the Round-Up, Pendleton, Oregon.
Copyrighted by O. G. Allen.

Try This: Before reading *Let 'Er Buck!*, use the glossary at the back of the book to have students illustrate the vocabulary words' definitions. As you read, have them hold up the vocabulary card with their illustration.

The National Cowboy Museum website

PERSON 3

Mary Fields (1832–1914)

 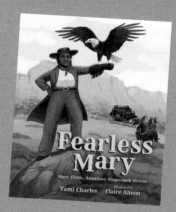

Nickname: Stagecoach Mary

Job: Mail carrier, freight hauler, forewoman, cook, carpenter, wood chopper, and farmer

Did You Know? Mary Fields was the first African American woman to work for the U.S. Postal Service. She also loved baseball!

For More Info: Read *The True West* (cited earlier) and *Fearless Mary: Mary Fields, American Stagecoach Driver*, written by Tami Charles and illustrated by Claire Almon. You can learn more about Mary Fields on the National Postal Museum website.

Try This: Explore more about what life in Montana was like during Fields's lifetime. Have students think about and chart the kind of weather and animals from which Fields had to protect the mail.

The National Postal Museum website

Tips for Designing Your Own Powerful People Sets

You can create Powerful People Sets about a variety of topics and for a variety of purposes. Maybe you want a set of mathematicians or scientists to align with an upcoming unit. You could even have your students make their own Powerful People Sets for an area of individual or class interest. Designing Powerful People Sets is a great way to deepen students' understanding of historical figures they already know as well as to introduce them to people they may never have heard of.

In addition, you can use the Powerful People Sets template as a tool not only in your teaching but also for your own teacher learning. This template can also be found in the appendix.

Ways to Find Your People

Listed here are a few resources that can help you as you begin to learn more about important people in Black history and to create sets of people to study together.

Social Media

Social media has become an educational tool that I lean on when conducting Black history research. I have gained a lot of Black history knowledge by following and engaging with people on Instagram, Tik Tok, and Twitter.

> **Ernest Crim III** (@mrcrim3 on Instagram and TikTok) shares and teaches Black history. He is also the author of *Black History Saved My Life: How My Viral Hate Crime Led to an Awakening*.

> **Leo Glazé** (@IAmLeoGlaze on Twitter) is an ethnic studies/history educator who shares and teaches Black history.

> **Erica Buddington** (@ericabuddington on Twitter) is a Black history educator and the founder of Langston League (@LangstonLeague on Twitter), which is a curriculum collective at the intersection of Black history, culture, and accessibility, designing instructional materials for K–12 students, film, and TV.

A Powerful People Set About _____

BIG IDEA: What do these people have in common? What makes them fit with the big idea of the set?

PEOPLE: Find three to five people who fit with the big idea of this set. List their names and dates of birth and death (if applicable).				

JOB, CAREER, INVENTION, KNOWN FOR: This section will change depending on the big idea of the set. Be sure to list as much information as you can so as to avoid the danger of a repeated narrative.				

DID YOU KNOW? As you research, what sticks out to you, and what might grab the attention of your students? What might be an important piece of information about the person that isn't well known or understood?

FOR MORE INFO: This is the space to list other resources for learning about the people in your set. These resources can include books, photographs, videos, interviews, songs, exhibits, and so on.

TRY THIS: As you're researching and exploring resources, think about an activity or task that will enable students to process and apply the information they're learning about the people in the set.

ALWAYS KEEP IN MIND . . . These Powerful People Sets cannot "cover" a person or a group of people's entire history. The information in these charts comprises only bits and pieces of the lives they lived, not their whole story. I challenge you to discover and learn more on your own and with your students. Use these charts as starting points, be careful of those repeated narratives, and remember to tell the truth, as fully as you can.

Children's Books

Children's books that center Black historical figures are great resources to get you started. You can use these books as a way to launch into deeper research about the people and events featured in the text.

Who Are Your People?, written by Bakari Sellers and illustrated by Reggie Brown

Bakari Sellers takes a journey with his twins as they learn who their people are. They learn about their strength, persistence, and resistance and see people such as Muhammad Ali, John Lewis, Harriet Tubman, and a Buffalo soldier.

Your Legacy: A Bold Reclaiming of Our Enslaved History, written by Schele Williams and illustrated by Tonya Engel

This book takes readers on a journey from past to present. The book highlights the determination, ingenuity, brilliance, and strength of African Americans such as James Baldwin, Robert Smalls, Madam C. J. Walker, and focuses on ancestors and the love and courage they've passed down.

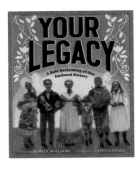

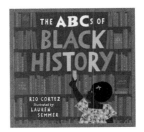

The ABC's of Black History, written by Rio Cortez and illustrated by Lauren Semmer

The ABC's of Black History is one of my favorite collections of Black histories. Each letter in the book highlights multiple Black histories and celebrates the beauty of Blackness. Whereas the Black Panther Party is often left out of resources for children, this picture book makes *P* for *Panther* and shares information about Huey P. Newton and the power of the movement.

Finding Your People

"Who are your people?" Bakari Sellers poses this question in his book by the same name. This picture book follows him and his twins as they take a journey to see who their people are. "Your people were fighters. When they were told they had to leave because of the color of their skin, they sat down" (Sellers 2022). Sellers encourages readers to feel pride in who they are, where they come from, and who their people are. As you learn about Black history and as you create learning experiences for your students, I hope that you too can find some of that same pride Bakari Sellers expresses.

Black history is so much richer, deeper, and more diverse than what you may have been taught in school. You may feel overwhelmed by how much you don't yet know, but don't let that stop you from beginning your learning journey— beginning to learn more yourself, beginning to teach more to your students.

What I have shared with you in this chapter is the result of years of research, developing activities, teaching in classrooms, and "finding my people"— people who interest me, people who interest my students, and people who I notice are missing from curriculum materials.

I invite you to think about what you are interested in and what your students are interested in. If it's art, there is so much to learn from Gordon Parks, Alma Thomas, and Kehinde Wiley. If it's engineering, get to know Elijah McCoy, Frederick McKinley Jones, and Annie Easley. If you're into music, Duke Ellington, Aretha Franklin, and Ella Fitzgerald are perfect for you. And you must meet Earyn McGee if you're into reptiles. Whatever your passion is, with Black history, you will find your people. Sometimes they find you, but often-times, you have to go out and find them. They are waiting for you.

Beyond the Books

2

I do not think that young readers are too tender for tough topics. Even before "anti-racist" was a term, my books highlighted social justice issues and engaged students in critical literacy.

—Carole Boston Weatherford, in an interview about her children's book *Unspeakable* (2021)

"What happened before Martin Luther King Jr.?" Ezra, a kindergartener in my class, asked.

"What do you mean?" I responded, confused.

"What were Black people doing before they started marching? What was happening to them?" Ezra continued.

"Well," I said, not knowing exactly where or how to begin, "there was a lot going on before Martin Luther King Jr., and Black people have done a lot—before and after Martin Luther King Jr."

"Like what?" Ezra nudged, in the way kindergartners beautifully do, refusing to let go of a question until they are really and truly satisfied with the answer.

I paused. How could I answer such a big question honestly and fully? How could I honor Ezra's brilliant thinking? I could have given a quick response and left it alone, but I could tell that Ezra, and the rest of the class watching our exchange, were looking for more than that. They were in search of more, and they deserved more. I had introduced my students to King and other leaders of the Civil Rights Movement, but they wanted to know even more. And they expected me to have the answers!

"You know what?" I said to Ezra and the rest of my students. "I actually have a few books that we can pull out tomorrow to answer some of your questions."

"Can we all read them, Ms. James?" piped in Caroline, who had been listening intently.

"Of course!"

And do you know what those students came into our classroom looking for the very next day at school? They came ready to look at those books we talked about. They came ready to explore. They came ready for answers, and I knew the best places to get them.

Children's Books as Places to Begin

Children's books do more than tell stories. They provide information, ignite discussions, and answer questions. And although we still have a long way to go, more and more brilliant and beautiful picture books are being published that represent Black histories, characters, and stories. It is helpful to consider the different kinds of children's books we read to our students and make available to them in our classrooms. Within the broad topic of Black history, the goal is to have a diverse range of genres, topics, and themes represented.

As you select books, it is important to keep in mind the words of Dr. Rudine Sims Bishop:

> Books are sometimes windows, offering views of worlds that may be real or imagined, familiar or strange. These windows are also sliding glass doors, and readers have only to walk through in imagination to become part of whatever world has been created or recreated by the author. When lighting conditions are just right, however, a window can also be a mirror (1990, ix).

Whether the books we choose mirror the histories of our students or their ancestors or are windows or sliding glass doors to histories that were previously unfamiliar to them, the work we do to provide high-quality and representative texts to our students is critical.

Further, we want to be aware of who is telling the story in the texts we select for our classrooms. Who are the author and illustrator? How and why are they suited to tell the stories in the books they create? What research did they engage in order to make their books? How do they point readers to where they can learn more? Consider centering #OwnVoices texts ("a term credited to author Corinne Duyvis, who suggested the hashtag on Twitter in 2015 to 'recommend kidlit about diverse characters written by authors from that same diverse group'" [Yorio 2018]).

Here are a few categories I find helpful as I glance across my classroom library and make selections for new books to bring into my classroom:

Type of Children's Book That Centers Black Histories and Stories	A Few Examples
Biographies that tell about a person's whole life or an important moment or period in their life.	*A Nation's Hope: The Story of Boxing Legend Joe Louis*, written by Matt de la Peña and illustrated by Kadir Nelson *Coretta Scott*, written by Ntozake Shange and illustrated by Kadir Nelson *R-E-S-P-E-C-T: Aretha Franklin, the Queen of Soul*, written by Carole Boston Weatherford and illustrated by Frank Morrison
Books that tell about a historical event or time period.	*Sugar Hill: Harlem's Historic Neighborhood*, written by Carole Boston Weatherford and illustrated by R. Gregory Christie *Evicted! The Struggle for the Right to Vote*, written by Alice Faye Duncan and illustrated by Charly Palmer *Freedom Soup*, written by Tami Charles and illustrated by Jacqueline Alcántara
Books that tell stories of Black joy and childhood. These books may be fiction or nonfiction, set in the past or present.	*I Am Every Good Thing*, written by Derrick Barnes and illustrated by Gordon C. James *Princess Hair* by Sharee Miller *M Is for Melanin: A Celebration of the Black Child* by Tiffany Rose

continues

Type of Children's Book That Centers Black Histories and Stories	A Few Examples
Browsable nonfiction books—"readers can easily dip in and out . . . focusing on the sections that interest them the most, or they can read the books cover to cover (Emmett 2012)" (Stewart and Correia, 2021, 14-15).	*The ABCs of Black History*, written by Rio Cortez and illustrated by Lauren Semmer *Brave. Black. First.: 50+ African American Women Who Changed the World*, written by Cheryl Willis Hudson and illustrated by Erin K. Robinson *Woke: A Young Poet's Call to Justice*, written by Mahogany L. Browne with Elizabeth Acevedo and Olivia Gatwood and illustrated by Theodore Taylor III

Three Ways to Go Beyond the Book

For us to know what questions books answer, we teachers have to read the book! We have to get to know the book. And we must go beyond the book.

What do I mean by going beyond the book—isn't reading it enough? In some cases, yes. But when it comes to gathering information for students and teaching Black histories, we must go a little deeper than that.

In their article, "Reading Beyond the Book with Primary Sources," Noreen Naseem Rodríguez, Anna Falkner, and Elizabeth Tetu Bohl perfectly sum up the purposes of going beyond the book:

> Sharing primary sources about a specific event or place before reading a book aloud may elicit students' wonderings about a topic and can establish the connections students make to previous experiences in their communities and in school. Inserting primary sources in the middle of a read-aloud can juxtapose the events of a text with different actors, settings, or moments in time, allowing students to make comparisons and contrasts between the visual and written text of the book and the contents of the primary. Sharing primary sources after a read-aloud can offer greater context to the narrative found in the story and may launch student investigations into areas of further interest. (2022, 749)

Let's take a look at three strategies I use to go beyond the book as I plan for read-alouds with my students. There is no true order for these strategies, and oftentimes they will overlap. Although I list some teacher questions that may be helpful for each strategy, the questions are interchangeable.

Three Strategies for Going Beyond the Book When Preparing to Teach Black History

I recommend reading this section with a Black history picture book in hand. Whether it is one you have already read or one you just purchased, practicing these strategies will help you get familiar with the text and anticipate how you might use it in the classroom.

Previewing the Book

When previewing a book, you are becoming familiar with the book as an educator. You may want to take note of pages that resonate with you, questions you have, vocabulary that may be new to students, and impactful illustrations.

> **Questions to Ask Ourselves as We Preview Texts Before We Read Them with Students**
>
> * What stands out to me as I read?
> * What might students notice during the read-aloud?
> * Where might I plan to pause for discussion during the read-aloud?
> * What questions or prompts for discussion might I use?

A Peek into My Classroom

When I previewed *The 1619 Project: Born on the Water*, written by Nikole Hannah-Jones and Renée Watson and illustrated by Nikkolas Smith, I noticed that there is a page in the book with no words, just the illustration of a ship, the *White Lion*. I placed a sticky note on this page because I wanted to pause as we were reading and ask my students why they thought there were no words on the page. On the pages just prior to the ship image, there are two poems, "Stolen" and "The White Lion," that tell readers how Africans were stolen from their homes and forced onto ships. These pages of *Born on the Water* mark a dramatic shift in tone (both in words and illustrations) from the beginning of the book, which details the lives of Africans prior to 1619. Pages that make us pause as teacher readers are often places we might ask students to pause as well. They may notice the same things we have noticed, and oftentimes they notice additional details we may have missed.

Reading Between the Lines

In books about Black history, it is common for there to be outside references present in the text—maybe the title of a song, the name of a historical figure, or a description of an event. These are references you might take note of and look up as you read between the lines. Take the time to find those images, songs, people, or events and share them with students.

Questions to Ask Ourselves as We Read Between the Lines

* What parts of the book will my students be curious about? What will they be potentially confused by?

* Are there resources I might gather about someone or something mentioned in the text or represented in the illustrations?

* What activities could I provide my students to help enhance their understanding of the ideas in the book?

A Peek into My Classroom

Let the Children March, written by Monica Clark-Robinson and illustrated by Frank Morrison, is a book that captures the events of the Children's Crusade in Birmingham, Alabama, in 1963. The text in the book mentions a few songs, including "Ain't Gonna Let Nobody Turn Me Around" and "We Shall Overcome." In my class, we use the book and the song lyrics as paired texts to better understand the events depicted in *Let the Children March*. For example,

we thought together about the song title "Ain't Gonna Let Nobody Turn Me Around" paired with the illustration from the book shown here. I asked students, "Why would the marchers be singing 'Ain't Gonna Let Nobody Turn Me Around'? What would that mean to them?"

Researching Beyond the Book

Take all the information you've gathered from the "Previewing a Book" and "Reading Between the Lines" strategies and keep learning. While reading between the lines often involves finding outside resources to further investigate someone or something mentioned in the text, researching beyond the book takes this work a step further. For example, you might research the time period in which the book takes place to give yourself and your students a better idea of the context surrounding the story. Sometimes picture books spark questions that can't be answered in the text and prompt inquiry beyond the book.

Questions to Ask Ourselves as We Research Beyond the Book

* What do I need to know in order to answer the questions my students might have? How can I prepare?

* What outside resources (photos, song lyrics, timelines, other books, artifacts, interviews, videos, etc.) might enhance students' understanding of the book's topic?

* What activities could I provide my students to help enhance their understanding of the ideas in the book?

A Peek into My Classroom

Ethel L. Payne, also known as the First Lady of the Black Press, was a journalist and activist. In the picture book *The Power of Her Pen*, written by Lesa Cline-Ransome and illustrated by John Parra, we learn about Payne's work in the White House, her interviews with soldiers overseas, and her work with the newspaper the *Chicago Defender*. For my youth program, The Black History Club, I paired the reading of *The Power of Her Pen* with artifacts I found through my own research to bring Payne's story to life for my students. I shared with them that the *Chicago Defender* still exists as a newspaper today, and we were able to view it online. I also shared photos of Ethel Payne interviewing Black soldiers in Vietnam and with presidents Lyndon B. Johnson and Richard Nixon. These artifacts helped students create a mental timeline of Payne's life and provided further context for her story.

Putting It All Together with *Moses*

Any time I read a book with my students, there is always a purpose. *Moses: When Harriet Tubman Led Her People to Freedom* (Figure 2.1), written by Carole Boston Weatherford and illustrated by Kadir Nelson, is a book that takes more than a day to read with my students. We really take our time with the text, and I give my students time to process what we are reading. In the next sections you will see how I go beyond the book with *Moses* by previewing the book, reading between the lines, and doing research on key concepts in the text. Although I do not always engage with all the strategies for going beyond the book with each title we read, certain foundational texts that I know we will want to return to again and again are worth this effort.

Previewing with *Moses*

Pausing for discussion on pages with impactful illustrations is a powerful strategy for helping students truly understand moments in Black history. In order to choose where I want to pause, I read *Moses* from cover to cover and made notes of what I noticed as I previewed the book.

In this book, there is an image of Harriet Tubman stepping into a body of water after receiving guidance from a woman in a wagon (Figure 2.2)—an illustration that stood out to me because it sparked the memory of baptisms at church when I was a young child. The congregation would sing "Wade in the Water" during the procession of the people who were getting baptized. It was a song that we sang low and slow, and, honestly, when I first heard it as a young child, it creeped me out! But as I grew up, learned, and researched, I understood why we sang "Wade in the Water," and its connection to the Black church.

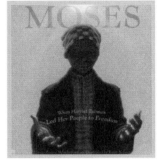

FIGURE 2.1. *Moses,* written by Carole Boston Weatherford and illustrated by Kadir Nelson

FIGURE 2.2. A page from *Moses* that depicts Harriet Tubman wading into the water as she journeys to freedom.

When previewing this book before reading it to my students, I knew that the page on which Harriet enters the water was one place I'd want to pause. When we got to that page, I asked students the open-ended question "What do you see?" Up to this point in the book, we know that Harriet is escaping enslavement and headed to freedom. We know that she doesn't want to get caught and that she has to be quiet. When we first view this illustration as a class, my young students often make connections to their own very different experiences with water—for example, swimming, fishing, or being on a boat in a lake. Because many students may have a limited understanding of slavery and the time period in which Harriet Tubman lived, I ask them whether Harriet is having those same experiences. We talk about how she is getting into the water. Is she splashing? Is she playing? How might she feel? How does the illustrator show her wading into the water? This illustration and the discussion we have around it gives students insight into Harriet's dangerous journey and shows them the strategies used and great risk undertaken to escape slavery.

Another part of my previewing process for this book was reading the book's foreword, written by the author, and gathering background knowledge about the time period in which Harriet Tubman lived. I also chose to read this foreword to my students to share this same background knowledge with them. Although not every picture book includes a foreword, many picture books with a historical focus do include extra background material or peritext, such as timelines, author's notes, maps, and historical photographs. Make sure to dig into these resources that have been curated with intention by the author, and consider ways to share them with your students.

Reading Between the Lines with *Moses*

When I read any picture book, I am always thinking about ideas for activities to go along with the book that will extend my students' learning about and understanding of the topic. Books about Black history are no different. As I read I am constantly asking myself, What could we do with this book? How can I help my students further process the content in the text? I want these activities to be age-appropriate and meaningful.

I believe that read-alouds, especially with young children, should be as interactive as possible. This can mean posing questions for students to discuss, analyzing illustrations, and integrating art. These interactive activities may occur before, during, and/or after our read-alouds.

For *Moses*, I chose to do an interactive activity at a pausing point during reading. When we get to the illustration of Harriet Tubman getting into the water, and after our discussion of this page, I ask my students to form a circle and sit down. I join the circle too, and place the book in front of me. I ask my students to share again how Harriet enters the water and why she does it that way. I invite the students to drum their hands on their legs and follow my beat pattern. We do this for a few seconds, and usually they end up speeding up the beat. I remind them to slow down, telling them that I am going to teach them a song about wading in the water, wading as Harriett did. I ask them whether my song is going to be loud, and they always answer with no, it has to be low. I tell them to echo me as I sing and to keep the slow beat. Together, we sing the chorus of "Wade in the Water" in call-and-response form. After we sing the chorus a few times, we stop, and I ask them again why Harriet had to wade.

The following day during our literacy time, I pass copies of the "Wade in the Water" lyrics and assign high-frequency words (such as *in* and *the*) that appear in the song for them to highlight or circle (Figure 2.3). As they do this work, I play the song at a low volume in the background. Having an opportunity to see and hear the song again allows students more time to process the lyrics and connect to the meaning (with the added literacy bonus of practicing reading high-frequency words!).

This same activity can also be done with the spiritual "Go Down Moses." You might also read more about this song as a class, decipher the code in the song, and talk about its history and meaning.

The purpose of reading between the lines is to help students process the book and to model how to dig deeper into a text to learn more about the topic at hand.

FIGURE 2.3. Students find and build high-frequency words from the lyrics of "Wade in the Water" as they listen to the song.

Researching Beyond the Book with *Moses*

For this particular book, some of my research into Harriet Tubman's life came right from the book's foreword. As I was reading this section of the book, I pulled out some key vocabulary and concepts, such as the Underground Railroad, African American spirituals and their coded messages, and how states legally forbade African Americans from learning to read and write. I also found a photograph of Harriet Tubman that I could show my students. With that context in mind, I continued my research by seeking out other sources of information on these topics. I knew I wouldn't be able to learn everything, but learning more would enable me to help my students find answers to their own questions as well. I wanted to have as much knowledge as possible about the time period in which Harriet Tubman lived in order to "set the scene" for my students, to help them better understand her life and the lives of all those who were enslaved and fought for their freedom.

I educated myself so that I could educate my students. I wanted to be prepared to answer any questions while also explaining my answers with details and examples. When going beyond the book, you may choose just one of these strategies. But if you are digging deeply into a person or topic, you might choose to use all three.

Book Collections

Essentially, a book collection is a set of texts that have one or more commonalities—a stack of books that connect to one another in some way. When I was learning how to teach literacy in my teaching program, we learned a lot about doing author and illustrator studies and creating stacks of mentor texts for these studies. These author and illustrator studies consisted of reading as many books as possible by the same author or the same illustrator and studying some aspect of their craft. These studies in elementary schools often include books by classic authors such as Jan Brett, Steve Jenkins, Lois Ehlert, Eric Carle, and Gail Gibbons (all white authors, we might note). In more recent years, I've noticed teachers being more inclusive with their author/illustrator studies (as well as when it comes to building their classroom libraries), including studies of Jacqueline Woodson, Christian Robinson, Matt de la Peña, Oge Mora, and Grace Lin.

As I began buying and receiving books that focused on Black history, I noticed that many of them could be sorted or categorized as though I were building a stack of books for an author/illustrator study. And while many of my books could be sorted by author or illustrator, I also noticed that there were many more connections between books than just having been written or illustrated by the same person. For instance, many of my books featured activists, leaders, historical events, innovators, or biographies. Yes, some of those collections overlap (which I love!), but they could also stand alone as a collection to be studied by students just as we might study a set of books in an author/illustrator study.

Why Curate Book Collections?

I curate book collections because I have noticed that we too often read one book and think we are done learning or that we "know enough." We paint one narrative of a person or historical event and think we know all there is to know. If my students have questions (as all students do!), I want to provide as many resources as possible. I want these resources to be accessible for them to grab, hold, and get to know. For example, when we study the Civil Rights Movement, I want to broaden our understanding of this movement and who was involved by reading such books as *Pies from Nowhere: How Georgia Gilmore Sustained the Montgomery Bus Boycott*, *R-E-S-P-E-C-T*, and *Lift as You Climb*. Learning about the women portrayed in these books helps students create not only a timeline of events but a fuller picture of what was going on.

My hope is that you can see the beauty in each of the collections that I describe in this chapter and that you use these resources in your classroom as learning tools for yourself and your students. I also hope that you use these collections as a jumping-off point for creating your own collections that intersect with your curriculum or are inspired by your students' interests and questions. Give them (and yourself!) space and time to explore and learn. What follows are a few book collections I curated for my classroom library.

Africa Collection

In the United States, we are often presented with a one-dimensional narrative about Africa. People often refer to Africa as a single country, when it is actually a continent composed of fifty-five different countries. We often reference the animals in parts of Africa, but know very little about the people who live there. And we rarely see images that illustrate the true diversity of Africa's people, countries, geography, and cultures. The books in this collection focus on both celebrating the beauty of Africa and honoring the continent as a place of origin for Black people, culture, and history.

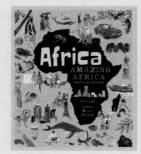

Africa, Amazing Africa: Country by Country, written by Atinuke and illustrated by Mouni Feddag

Africa, Amazing Africa focuses on the fifty-five countries in Africa, with detailed illustrations and information about each country.

Nelson Mandela by Kadir Nelson

In *Nelson Mandela*, author/illustrator Kadir Nelson beautifully details the story of Mandela's life and his mission to make change in South Africa.

Timelines from Black History: Leaders, Legends, Legacies

Timelines from Black History focuses on Black history across the diaspora with detailed illustrations and facts. This is a browsable book you can revisit again and again.

The 1619 Project: Born on the Water, written by Nikole Hannah-Jones and Renée Watson and illustrated by Nikkolas Smith

Using poetry and poignant illustrations, authors Nikole Hannah-Jones and Renée Watson and illustrator Nikkolas Smith tell the story of a young girl who receives a school assignment to research her family tree. With the help of her family, the girl learns the story of her ancestors, their lives in Africa, and how they were stolen from their home by slave traders. She learns about how her ancestors survived, fought, and live on through their descendants today.

From the Heart of Africa: A Book of Wisdom, collected by Eric Walters

This book of wisdom is a collection of aphorisms, or popular sayings, from countries across Africa. Paired with beautiful illustrations, this book celebrates African cultures and history.

Freedom over Me: Eleven Slaves, Their Lives, and Dreams Brought to Life by Ashley Bryan

Ashley Bryan uses historical documents, paintings, and poetry to bring to life and humanize the lives of enslaved Africans and tell the story of how their lives were forcibly altered when they were taken from their homes in Africa.

Where Do I Start?

Start with *Africa, Amazing Africa*. This book explores each country of Africa, celebrating what makes it unique. Once you've found a country of interest, go beyond the book to find other resources, photos, and information to share with your class.

Going Beyond

There is so much you can do with this entire collection or even with a single title. When introducing students to Africa, I like to start by asking them what they already know (or think they know) about the continent. I draw a huge outline of Africa and place it on the board or easel. I chart students' responses to my question before we begin exploring books and other resources. Once we've charted what we know, I begin reading books, showing pictures, sharing videos and songs, and introducing them to different people and specific countries that disrupt that single narrative they may have of Africa. Sharing the different climates, available natural resources, and technology presents Africa as a present, living continent instead of a place where only animals live.

Some teachers may have the space in their curriculum to dive into a full unit on Africa, while many will do this work by making connections between their standards/curriculum and the goal of a more robust understanding of Africa. There are many ways to integrate learning about Africa into lessons across the content areas. Science units can be a perfect place to introduce students to amazing animals such as the African penguin or the many species of butterfly that live on the continent. When my class was learning about force and motion in kindergarten, *The Boy Who Harnessed the Wind*, written by William Kamkwamba and Bryan Mealer and illustrated by Elizabeth Zunon, was the perfect book to show problem solving and a real-world application of scientific concepts through the eyes of a boy living in the country of Malawi.

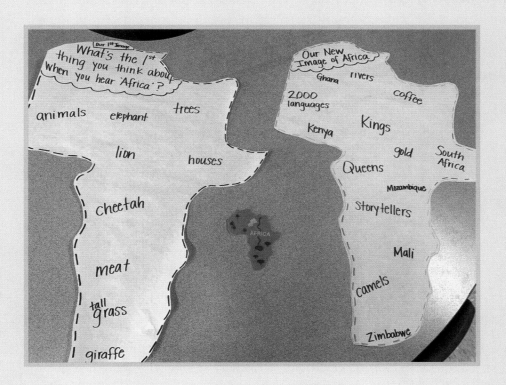

Inventors and Inventions Collection

Books about Black inventors and inventions make up a growing collection in my personal library, and they hold a special place in my heart. Highlighting Black inventors and inventions throughout history enables students to see the innovation, creativity, and contributions of Black people to the world around us. And while some of the inventors have passed on, their legacies are alive and well today through their inventions. Since I've begun building this collection, more and more books have been written about Black inventors and their inventions. This collection features different inventors from different times in history and introduces readers to a variety of inventions.

What Color Is My World? The Lost History of African-American Inventors, written by Kareem Abdul-Jabbar with Raymond Obstfeld and illustrated by Ben Boos and A. G. Ford

What Color Is My World? explores the history of Black inventors and their inventions through the story of a set of twins and a handyman working on their new home.

The Boy Who Harnessed the Wind, written by William Kamkwambda and Bryan Mealer and illustrated by Elizabeth Zunon

The Boy Who Harnessed the Wind tells the amazing true story of how fourteen-year-old William Kamkwambda used the resources around him to bring electricity to his Malawi village in the midst of a drought.

Have You Thanked an Inventor Today?, written by Patrice McLaurin and illustrated by Dian Wang

Have You Thanked an Inventor Today? follows the journey of a boy who learns about the history of Black inventors and their inventions throughout his day.

Whoosh! Lonnie Johnson's Super-Soaking Stream of Inventions, written by Chris Barton and illustrated by Don Tate

Whoosh! tells the story of inventor Lonnie Johnson and all of his many inventions, including the Super Soaker.

Where Do I Start?

In this collection, I suggest you start with *What Color Is My World?* and *Have You Thanked an Inventor Today?* These two books introduce a variety of different inventors and inventions. From there you can go beyond the book to find other texts and resources to dig deeper into a specific inventor or invention.

Going Beyond

One thing I love about studying inventors and inventions is that you can bring artifacts for your students to explore. A lunchbox, a bag of potato chips, hair care products, and an ice cream scoop are just a few items created by Black inventors that you might share with your students. For example, after reading *Whoosh!*, I give students time to talk about Lonnie Johnson's process for creating the Super Soaker. He did not get it right on the first try! Go beyond the book with that theme of perseverance by studying the inside covers to see the designs and sketches of Lonnie's other ideas and inventions. Reading this book is a great way to introduce students to the engineering design process and encourage them to create their own inventions.

Black Joy Collection

Black joy is an often overlooked part of Black history. We often teach students about hardships instead of triumphs, pain instead of glory. It is important that students have opportunities to see both the big historical moments of Black joy as well as its small everyday moments. This collection highlights the joys and beauties of Black history and Black childhood, and these books will be ones that your students cling to and want to read over and over again.

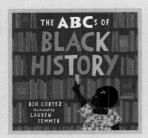

The ABCs of Black History, written by Rio Cortez and illustrated by Lauren Semmer

The ABCs of Black History is a collection of Black histories from A to Z—from *Anthem* to *Zenith*, from *Diaspora* to *Huey P. Newton*. A section at the end of the book gives more details about each Black history term and figure mentioned in the book.

Crown: Ode to the Fresh Cut, written by Derrick Barnes and illustrated by Gordon C. James

Crown celebrates the experience of getting a fresh haircut from the barbershop and the feelings that go along with it. This book is an exquisite illustration of the joy found in an everyday moment in childhood.

I Am Every Good Thing, written by Derrick Barnes and illustrated by Gordon C. James

Black boy joy is present throughout the text and illustrations of *I Am Every Good Thing*. This book shows the powerful, brave, loving, and true nature of Black boys and all that they are and can be.

M Is for Melanin: A Celebration of the Black Child by Tiffany Rose

M Is for Melanin is an alphabet book that is a true celebration of the Black child, from *A* is for *Afro* to *Z* is for *Zeal*. This book provides positive messages and affirmations and encourages all children to be who they are.

Brown: The Many Shades of Love, written by Nancy Johnson James and illustrated by Constance Moore

Brown focuses on the many shades of brown skin tones in a family. From chocolate to gingerbread, each brown is celebrated, and each brown is beautiful.

Where Do I Start?

The ABCs of Black History is a great starting point. This is a browsable book you can dip in and out of or read cover to cover. It highlights the glories of Black history and features terms, people, and events that are frequently left out of curricula, such as *diaspora*, *Huey P. Newton*, and *J'ouvert*. From there, use the other books to highlight the beauty of Black people from their skin to their hair, and have students share connections to their own lives.

Books from this collection are also great to read at the beginning of the school year as students are learning about one another and often exploring the concept of identity. I often begin the school year by having students create self-portraits, so these books are helpful mentor texts for my students to refer back to again and again as we engage in different activities and discussions of identity.

Going Beyond

What is melanin? If you read *M Is for Melanin*, that is a question students will want to know more about, so it's important to prepare for that as you preview the book and do your own research. Jot the answer on a sticky note in kid-friendly language and have other resources available from which students can learn more. Bring in other books about skin color, such as *All the Colors We Are: The Story of How Get Our Skin Color*, written by Katie Kissinger, with photographs by Chris Bohnhoff, which features great information about how our skin protects itself and what melanin is, and using maps explains how the sun affects people's skin color in different parts of the world. Celebrate the dreams, hopes, and futures of Black children with books such as *Dear Black Child*, written by Rahma Rodaah and illustrated by Lydia Mba, and *Hold Them Close: A Love Letter to Black Children*, written by Jamilah Thompkins-Bigelow and illustrated by Patrick Dougher. These books truly give students (and even adults!) a deeper understanding of melanin.

Historical Events Collection

History can be complex for young students (and even adults!) to grasp. Dates, historical figures, and events can be a lot for young children to make sense of when they are still developing an understanding of time and the concept of past versus present. Sometimes even last week can seem like history to young children! Yet when children are given the opportunity to build historical understandings over time, they are quite capable of comprehending big ideas and making connections between the past and today. This collection of books helps students create a mental (or physical, if you choose) timeline of some Black historical events.

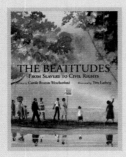

The Beatitudes: From Slavery to Civil Rights, written by Carole Boston Weatherford and illustrated by Tim Ladwig

The Beatitudes focuses on the role of African Americans' faith as the reader journeys through multiple Black histories to create a timeline.

All Different Now: Juneteenth, the First Day of Freedom, written by Angela Johnson and illustrated by E. B. Lewis

All Different Now tells the story of a girl and her community learning about the Emancipation Proclamation two years after the fact. In this story of the first Juneteenth, Johnson illuminates the significance of the date and the hopes for the freedom it brought to enslaved people.

Freedom Soup, written by Tami Charles and illustrated by Jacqueline Alcántara

Freedom Soup is a celebratory story of a grandmother, Ti Gran, and her granddaughter, Belle, making the traditional Haitian New Year's meal of Freedom Soup. As they cook together, Ti Gran shares the story of the Haitian Revolution and independence with her granddaughter as they celebrate freedom, traditions, and family.

Let the Children March, written by Monica Clark-Robinson and illustrated by Frank Morrison

Let the Children March tells the story of the 1963 Children's Crusade in Birmingham, Alabama. The illustrations show the experience of the children as they marched for equal rights and change.

A Day for Rememberin': Inspired by the True Events of the First Memorial Day, written by Leah Henderson and illustrated by Floyd Cooper

A Day for Rememberin' is inspired by the events of the first Memorial Day and the reason for this holiday. A glimpse into a seldom talked about history, this book highlights the work of African Americans to celebrate and honor Black soldiers.

A Song for the Unsung: Bayard Rustin, the Man Behind the 1963 March on Washington, written by Carole Boston Weatherford and Rob Sanders and illustrated by Byron McCray

A Song for the Unsung centers civil and gay rights activist Bayard Rustin and his journey from childhood to his pivotal role in organizing the March on Washington for Jobs and Freedom. Using song titles, the authors travel between past and present to show Bayard's agency, resilience, and perseverance.

Where Do I Start?

For this collection, I would start with *The Beatitudes*. This book offers a great overview of Black historical events and highlights such moments as the creation of Black churches and the funeral of Emmett Till, and gives information about Fannie Lou Hamer.

Going Beyond

I read *A Day for Rememberin'* with my kindergartners as part of our social studies unit on celebrations and holidays. Because there is a lot of text in the book, we spent two days reading the book together and studying its illustrations. Before we read the book, I shared an image of a painting titled *Red, White and Weary Blues* by Kadir Nelson (Figure 2.4), which can also be found in the book *The Undefeated*, written by Kwame Alexander and illustrated by Kadir Nelson. I posed the question, "What do you see?" to my students, and they had a number of responses as shown in the photo.

The students also commented on what the soldier was wearing and noticed a badge, sash, and belt, and that he was holding the American flag.

My goal in choosing to discuss this image was to humanize the soldiers about whom we were going to be reading and learning in *A Day for Rememberin'*. I hoped that as we read, students would have a visual of the kind of soldier the Black residents of Charleston, South Carolina, were honoring on the first Memorial Day.

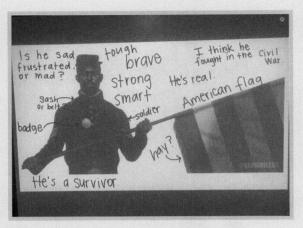

FIGURE 2.4 Students notice and wonder about *Red, White and Weary Blues*, a painting by Kadir Nelson, before reading *A Day for Rememberin'*.

As a way to remember the events of the first Memorial Day, we as a class came up with images that we thought represented the most important parts of the holiday. We thought it made sense to have an image of flowers, a soldier, a flag, a photo of Black children who participated in the first Memorial Day (which we saw at the back of the book), and a tombstone (Figure 2.5). I also wrote down words from the text that we felt were relevant, such as *Civil War, Decoration Day, Memorial Day*, and *Charleston, South Carolina (1865)*. The next day, we used envelopes to create an American flag and placed those images and symbols inside the flag envelope. I also found an article from Newsela about the first Memorial Day, and because the book mentioned the song "Nobody Knows the Trouble I've Seen," I printed off those lyrics and had my students find high-frequency words throughout the lyrics. All of those different components and resources helped me teach a full history of Memorial Day and enabled my students to see this one event in a variety of ways.

History is a major component of the elementary social studies curriculum, and using accessible children's books is an excellent way to teach

FIGURE 2.5. Students study several texts as they learn about Memorial Day.

these history standards. Whether your standards include comparing the past and the present or researching historical figures who have influenced our country, there is something to be found in these books. Go beyond highlighting Martin Luther King Jr.'s "I Have a Dream" speech and Rosa Parks's work as an activist. Introduce your students to such activists as Fannie Lou Hamer or to histories such as the first Memorial Day or to Haitian New Year. Find those hidden gems of Black history in these books and bring them to the light.

How to Build a Black History Book Collection

I have been building my Black history library since my junior year of college, when I taught third and fourth graders about the Harlem Renaissance. My library has been growing ever since, but whether you have a large collection of books or are just starting out, there are always new titles for you to discover. Here are a few tips for getting started building your own collection of Black history–focused books.

Choose a Black History That Interests You

As I am writing this right now, I cannot choose a single Black history that interests me the most; there are so many to choose from! Cowboys were my obsession last summer, and now it's cuisine. But I also love learning about Black artists, and inventions and inventors will always be an all-time fave. I also want to know everything I can about Africa. Do you get my point?

Whatever history you feel drawn to, find those books. Reading multiple books about a historical figure or event or theme helps us layer and add nuance to our thinking about Black history. Just the act of reading about multiple Black histories or seeking out several resources around a particular part of history is a way of saying that Black histories are important, worthy of our attention, and worth digging into.

Find the Commonality Among Books

As you begin to read and select books, you may start to see common themes or ideas emerging. For example, after reading *Crown*, I remembered that I had two books written and illustrated by Sharee Miller that celebrate hair, *Don't Touch My Hair* and *Princess Hair*. These books became the beginning of a text set around hair (as part of a study of identity) and were a hit with students, who all found ways of connecting to this set.

A single title may end up being a part of multiple text sets around different topics or themes. For example, I sometimes read *Let the Children March* alongside books about Martin Luther King Jr. because he is featured in that book and the book is set during the Civil Rights Movement. But other times I read it when we learn about Ruby Bridges so that my students can better understand the ways children participated in the Civil Rights Movement. As you begin to see similarities and connections among books, start creating your own collections lists.

It is important to note that the resources that make up your collections may not always be picture books. Sometimes you may want to include a cookbook, chapter book, piece of art, or song. Whatever the topic, educate yourself and then find the resources to educate your students.

Keep an Eye Out for New Favorites!

As you read and share books, you and your students will notice some of the same authors and illustrators who have worked on multiple books about Black histories. For example, I had a class of kindergartners and first graders who could spot illustrations by Kadir Nelson from a mile away. And as a teacher, I know that I can truly depend on books written by Carole Boston Weatherford to deliver accurate information about different Black histories, whether about people or events. Keep an eye out for these authors and illustrators via their websites or social media accounts to see what they are currently working on and to get updates on book release dates. There are also great social media accounts that share a wide variety of diverse picture books, including books about Black histories.

Social media and book creators' own websites are great ways to find and stay connected with the latest titles from our favorite authors and illustrators.

Some of My Favorite Authors

* Derrick Barnes
* Vanessa Brantley-Newton
* Tami Charles
* Bryan Collier
* Nikki Grimes
* Leah Henderson
* Kadir Nelson
* Andrea Davis Pinkney
* Jamilah Thompkins-Bigelow
* Carole Boston Weatherford
* Schele Williams
* Jaqueline Woodson

Some of My Favorite Illustrators

* Ashley Bryan
* R. Gregory Christie
* Bryan Collier
* Floyd Cooper
* Shane W. Evans
* Vashti Harrison
* Ekua Holmes

* Gordon C. James
* E. B. Lewis
* Sharee Miller
* Frank Morrison
* Kadir Nelson
* Bryan Pinkney
* Lauren Semmer

Some of My Favorite Instagram Accounts

* @booksgrowminds
* @hereweread
* @kidlitincolor
* @lawrencedailylearning
* @leeandlow
* @literally_cultured
* @lulusbookjourney

* @jojos_book_club
* @simonkids
* @thebookwrangler
* @thetinyactivists
* @thetututeacher
* @wokekindergarten

Award Winners

* **Coretta Scott King Book Award.** Coretta Scott King was an author, activist, and civil rights leader. Her award honors authors and illustrators who write or illustrate the best African American literature for children.

* **Carter G. Woodson Book Award.** Carter G. Woodson was an author, historian, and teacher who made a point of celebrating the contributions of Black people. His establishment of Negro History Week led to Black History Month. The Carter G. Woodson Book Award focuses on promoting the writing and publishing of social studies books for young readers that accurately depict topics related to minorities and race.

Dawnavyn's Ultimate Black History Book Collection

This is the collection I've been building since my junior year of college, and it is constantly growing. I have used these children's books again and again with students to teach Black histories. See what collections you can create from this list!

The Undefeated, written by Kwame Alexander and illustrated by Kadir Nelson

Little Legends: Exceptional Men in Black History by Vashti Harrison with Kwesi Johnson

Little Leaders: Bold Women in Black History by Vashti Harrison

28 Days: Moments in Black History That Changed the World, written by Charles R. Smith Jr. and illustrated by Shane W. Evans

The Roots of Rap: 16 Bars on the 4 Pillars of Hip Hop, written by Carole Boston Weatherford and illustrated by Frank Morrison

Seven Spools of Thread: A Kwanzaa Story, written by Angela Shelf Medearis and illustrated by Daniel Minter

Heart and Soul: The Story of America and African Americans by Kadir Nelson

Coretta Scott, written by Ntozake Shange and illustrated by Kadir Nelson

Black Heroes: A Black History Book for Kids by Arlisha Norwood

The Power of Her Pen: The Story of Groundbreaking Journalist Ethel L. Payne, written by Lesa Cline-Ransome and illustrated by John Parra

Sugar Hill: Harlem's Historic Neighborhood, written by Carole Boston Weatherford and illustrated by R. Gregory Christie

We Are the Ship: The Story of Negro League Baseball by Kadir Nelson

Have I Ever Told You Black Lives Matter, written by Shani Mahiri King and illustrated by Bobby C. Martin Jr.

Let Freedom Sing by Vanessa Newton

Evicted! The Struggle for the Right to Vote, written by Alice Faye Duncan and illustrated by Charly Palmer

H Is for Harlem, written by Dinah Johnson and illustrated by April Harrison

Stand Up! 10 Mighty Women Who Made a Change, written by Brittney Cooper and illustrated by Cathy Ann Johnson

The People Remember, written by Ibi Zoboi and illustrated by Loveis Wise

Share Black Stories

There is a true love for Black history–focused books in my classroom. My students can access them on the shelf, read them with a buddy, and refer to them when making connections to other books we read.

I Am Every Good Thing is one such book that means a lot to my class (Figure 2.6). This is a book from our Black joy collection, one we read at the beginning of the year, on a rainy day, during morning meetings, in the middle of the year, during our unit on community, and at the very end of the year as a farewell and affirmation. I have found it in the writing center, a student's mailbox, and in the arms of a sleeping kindergartner in our classroom's safe place. It's a book in which my students see themselves and see their classmates, and they see Black histories. It is a book that affirms us, comforts us, and challenges us to remember who we are.

I'd love to be able to list every single book that highlights, celebrates, honors, or features Black histories, but that is the work of a lifetime. My hope is that you can find those books, create those collections, and read the books that benefit the education of your students, yourself, and the community of your classroom.

Books expose students to a fuller narrative of Black history. Not just the tragedy and the hardships but also the resistance. Not just the struggle and enslavement but the triumphs and successes, the innovation, brilliance, ingenuity, courage, intellect, and dignity. Books that center Black history aren't just for Black children; they are books for all children.

FIGURE 2.6. This is our favorite illustration from *I Am Every Good Thing*. It shows an image of past and present and perfectly illustrates the relationship we have to our ancestors. For us, these pages represented students in our classroom who looked similar to the boys in the foreground. They are also pages we used during our personal history study in social studies to support our definition of who our ancestors are, and the text was used as an affirmation of who we are and our role in our personal history.

Beyond the Curriculum

3

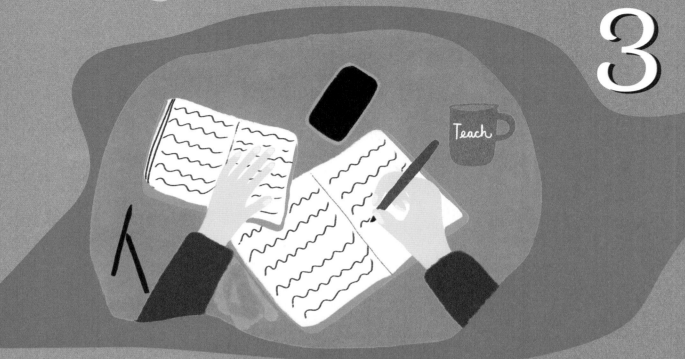

The absence of African Americans within the narrative of the founding of the U.S. curriculum is startling.

—Wayne Au, Anthony L. Brown,
and Dolores Calderón (2021, 144)

You can abide by state standards and teach Black histories.

I have worked in two different educational settings during my years of teaching early childhood and elementary school students. I spent my first years of teaching in a private school, which was also a laboratory school for the college from which I graduated. There, I taught in a multiage classroom with students ranging from kindergarten to fifth grade. Many teachers there had a master's degree in curriculum and instruction, and we took pride in creating purposeful inquiry-based curricula for our students. Our teaching was still guided by state standards, but we also had a great deal of autonomy in deciding which literacy, math, science, and social studies topics to teach and how to teach them, while also integrating art. With that experience, I was able to see how the curriculum could be revised to fit the needs of my students.

From there, I spent the next several years in a public school district teaching kindergarteners. As all public school teachers can attest, understanding and teaching the state standards was a critical part of my work. Yet I also knew it wasn't my only task. I knew, as I understood the standards and curricula I was expected to teach, that there would also be spaces for me to add to, revise, challenge, and disrupt the curriculum.

Now, I wasn't ripping pages out of the math, literacy, social studies, and science curricula. But I was reading through them with a different lens—a Black history lens. I wasn't reading the curriculum so that I could memorize the scripts provided; I was reading it to see what information was provided and what wasn't.

As you read your own curriculum and standards documents, consider asking yourself these questions:

* What standards and curricula am I responsible for teaching my students?
* Whose stories and voices are centered in this curriculum? Whose stories and voices are missing?
* What connections might I make between the curriculum as it is written and Black histories?
* How do the standards honor Black histories? What might I *add*, *revise*, *challenge*, or *disrupt* in order for our teaching and learning to honor Black histories?

Where's the Black History?

Think about those activities that you do in your classroom every year. In elementary school, many of those activities are accompanied by reading a book aloud. For example, I have a set of first-week-of-school books and activities that I must do. Before winter break, I have book collections, celebrations, and activities that I plan and save just for that time of year. And of course there are spring activities, end-of-year activities, and fall activities. There is a purpose for each of those activities and reasons why we do them at a specific time of year.

But when it comes to Black histories, February should not be the only time those books and activities are shared. Unlike those first-week-of-school activities, Black history does not have a season. In the words of Yolanda Sealey-Ruiz, "Black history cannot be contained" (2022). Black histories can fill any and all spaces throughout the curriculum. I know that this is true because I've spent years bringing Black histories into my classroom all year long.

I'm going to let you in on a little secret: your curriculum may not always reveal the ways in which the topics you teach connect to Black history. I have opened up the social studies curriculum and noticed that Black histories aren't featured. I have looked at science resources and noticed the lack of Black scientists featured. I have read through the literacy curriculum and have seen the absence of Black stories that feature Black characters and are written by Black authors.

And I know I am not alone in these realizations. "Decades of curriculum research have uncovered a persistent trend: white people are depicted as dominating the history of the United States, whereas communities of color and their experiences are omitted or misrepresented in social studies textbooks and curriculum standards" (An 2020, 4). We can't wait for standards, curricula, and textbooks to catch up and present more truthful history, to celebrate Black history. We must begin this work now.

Let's take a peek into four units I taught across the content areas in my classroom to see some ways we might add to, revise, challenge, and disrupt the curriculum in order to teach Black history throughout the year. While your standards, curriculum, and grade level may differ from mine, it is my hope that the stories and examples from these units inspire you as you do this work in your classroom and in the units you teach.

The Civics Unit: A Story of Starting with the Standards and Going Beyond Them

Where I teach, in the state of Missouri, one of our social studies standards asks elementary students to explore the "principles expressed in documents shaping constitutional democracy in the United States" (Missouri Department of Elementary and Secondary Education 2016, 2). For kindergarteners, this work includes a study of civics, individual rights, roles in the community, and rules. In my district's civics unit, we focus on the roles of children and adults at home and school as well as the rules students follow in both of these places. In past years, conversations with my kindergartners have led us to thinking together about rules of the road (wear your seatbelt, follow the speed limit), the importance of not taking things that aren't yours, and what happens when rules aren't followed.

The standards ask young children to understand that rules exist at home, in schools, and in the community for a reason and that we all need to follow these rules. And while the standard ends there, our teaching doesn't have to! Young children are often deeply interested in fairness, and they understand, even from a young age, that rules have nuance. They want to explore big questions such as "Are all rules good?" "Should we follow a rule if we think it is bad?" and "Who gets to make or change rules?"

Going Beyond the Standard with *Speak Up*

Speak Up, written by Miranda Paul and illustrated by Ebony Glenn, supports our conversations about rules in our communities and country by bringing nuance and a critical lens to the topic. The first few pages of this picture book illustrate some of the many ways and reasons why people use their voices to "speak up." When your name is mispronounced or when someone is spreading a rumor, you can speak up, the book tells us. Further into the book, a two-page spread that depicts portraits of Nelson Mandela, Malala Yousafzai, Martin Luther King Jr., and Ruth Bader Ginsburg reads, "When a rule just isn't fair or has gotten much too old—Work for change. Justice comes when we are bold" (Paul 2020). This statement challenges the notion (and the standard) that rules should always be accepted and followed.

My students are always particularly interested in talking about this spread that features the portraits of four adults who spoke up to change rules. As we linger over these pages, I ask my students, "Do you recognize anyone on these pages?" They are excited to engage with the pages, leaning in to study the illustrations.

"YES! That's Barack Obama!" Luke replies.

"Oh! Yes, this illustration sort of looks like him, but it's actually Nelson Mandela," I respond.

"Who is Nelson Mandela?" another student chimes in.

"Hey! She's wearing hijab!" Charlotte shouts out, pointing to another one of the portraits.

"Yeah—like the sister in *The Proudest Blue*," Kia adds.

"This is Malala Yousafzai," I say.

I give a few moments of space for students to notice details from these pages and add comments and questions.

The end pages of *Speak Up* list people—both children and adults—who have spoken up to create change in a variety of ways. Those end pages also list a number of ways we can take action right now and create change by making signs, emailing state representatives, and donating money. *Speak Up* offers many opportunities to dive deeper, make connections, and do further research, and I know we will return to this book many times throughout the year.

A Few More Books

No matter the grade you teach, social studies standards often include a study of civics, rules, and laws. These standards present us with the perfect opportunity to help students grapple with big questions such as "Should we always follow rules?" and "How can we change rules we think are unfair?" Here are a few more books in addition to *Speak Up* that I use to support this work:

Sometimes People March by Tessa Allen

Sofia Valdez, Future Prez, written by Andrea Beaty and illustrated by David Roberts

We the People: The United States Constitution Explored and Explained, written by Aura Lewis and Evan Sargent

Counting on Community by Innosanto Nagara

An ABC of Equality, written by Chana Ginelle Ewing and illustrated by Paulina Morgan

Get Up, Stand Up (adapted from the song by Bob Marley), written by Cedella Marley and illustrated by John Jay Cabuay

What could have been a quick and superficial study of rules ("We have rules in our schools, homes, and communities; we should all follow rules") was transformed by my students' interest in the idea that maybe not all rules were good ones—now or in the past—and the idea that they had the agency to advocate for changes to rules. As we continued this unit, I took the opportunity to make further connections to Black histories. I had already created a book collection for this unit, but after reading *Speak Up* and listening to my students' ideas and questions about rules, I added some other books to help us further explore this topic through the lens of Black history. I added *Let Freedom Sing* by Vanessa Newton (a book about the Civil Rights Movement); *Let the Children March*, written by Monica Clark-Robinson and illustrated by Frank Morrison (a book about the Children's March of 1963); and *Nelson Mandela* by Kadir Nelson. I wanted to dig deeper into that line in *Speak Up* about some rules being "unfair" and "much too old." These books provided an opportunity for students to begin to understand how laws and rules in our country and others (South Africa) were designed to separate people by race, and how both adults and children have fought and continue to fight to change these rules.

Talking About What We Can Do When Rules Aren't Fair

I taught this civics unit for three years in a kindergarten classroom, and each year the activities surrounding the topic changed. One year I chose to read *Peaceful Fights for Equal Rights*, written by Rob Sanders and illustrated by Jared Andrew Schorr, which features illustrations of the Greensboro sit-ins, Colin Kaepernick kneeling, and a variety of other ways to peacefully fight for equal rights. After reading, students created protest signs to speak up about something they believed in. Children chose the content for their posters and the messages they wrote on their signs. While some students argued lighter topics, such as "Kids should be able to wear makeup" and "Candy should be eaten before dinner," others wrote "Homeless/unhoused people should have homes," "Keep the ocean clean!," and "Black Lives Matter!" (Figure 3.1). As we made our signs, a student shared with the class that he had actually been to a protest and told his classmates about his experience.

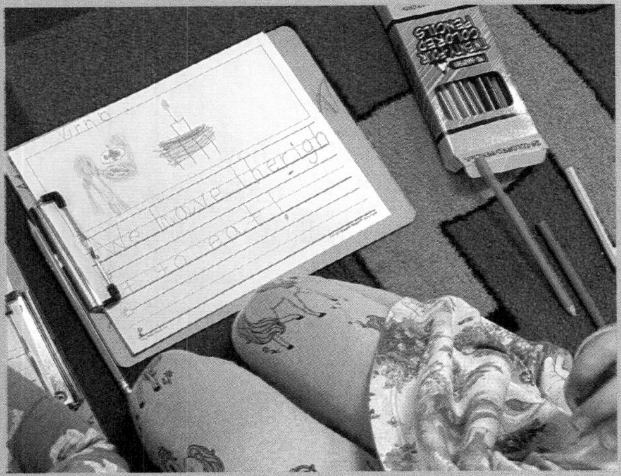

"What did you do at the protest?" I asked.

"I held up a sign and said 'NO JUSTICE! NO PEACE!'" he replied.

His classmates responded in recognition of this phrase by chanting, "No justice! No peace!"

Another year, as I was previewing the book, a page stood out to me and the sentence "Make buttons" sparked an idea. With the help of our amazing music and English language learner teachers, we did exactly

FIGURE 3.1. After reading *Peaceful Fights for Equal Rights*, students wrote about a right that they have. "We have the right to eat!" wrote one child.

what the book said. We. Made. Buttons. I asked students, "What is something that you love and think is important? Something that you want to share with other people on a button? Like the buttons I wear on my jacket." Just as with the protest signs, children chose the messages they wanted to put on their buttons, which included "Love is beautiful," "Peace," and "Protect the bees" (Figure 3.2).

Learning About Rules Through a Black History Lens

Even though the standards in our civics unit did not specifically include the idea of rules being broken or changed, I knew that this is a critical part of history and therefore decided to center it in our unit. The broad study of rules and laws offers us multiple opportunities to make connections to different time periods throughout history. This study of civics and rules helped my students to understand moments throughout Black history in which children and adults resisted unfair laws and fought to change them. I particularly wanted my students to understand the role that young activists have played in this work. Together as a class we learned about the Freedom Riders, young activists who, beginning in 1961, traveled on buses to southern states to protest the nonenforcement of laws that ruled segregation on public transportation unconstitutional. We studied the Children's March of 1963, in which young children marched to protest segregation (Figure 3.3). We also learned that most often, these activists' efforts were not celebrated. Freedom Riders were jailed. Police turned fire hoses and dogs on

FIGURE 3.2. A student wears buttons she made, which say "protect the bees" and "don't kill bees."

FIGURE 3.3. Before reading *Let the Children March* to kindergarteners, we looked at a historical photo from the Children's March of 1963 that is presented at the back of the book. I asked students what they saw in the photo and recorded their responses using Google Jamboard. Many students thought the people with the hose were putting out a fire. Later, when we read *Let the Children March*, my students were appalled to hear that the fire hose was being used to stop children from peacefully protesting. An understanding of resistance to rules being changed was an important part of our unit.

children in the Children's March, and many of them were even jailed. Change was not easy, and it was not immediate.

One year during this unit, as we were reading *Let the Children March*, one of my kindergarteners mentioned that sometimes people get shot for protesting.

"They better be careful. They gonna get shot for marching," she said.

"Why do you think that?" I responded.

"That's what they do on TV," she stated.

"I saw it on the news," another student added.

She saw it on TV. Even young students can and do make connections between history and current events. For these reasons, I make the choice not only to acknowledge when narratives are missing from curriculum but to include them, highlight them, and make it known to my students that Black histories exist and that history has a lot to teach us even if the standards won't.

Yes, all educators have standards and curricula they must teach, but it's up to you to decide how your students will go beyond what is printed in the curricular documents. My students will remember the books we read about rules, good and bad, and how people throughout history (and now) have fought to change unfair rules. They will remember the images of signs, kneeling, protests, unity, and boldness. They will remember that they made buttons to show others what it is they peacefully, or not so peacefully, fight for. While our work in this unit started from our state standards and district curricula, it evolved into a much fuller understanding of rules, whom they serve, and how we (children and adults alike) can be active and engaged members of the community.

Unspeakable: An Integrated Literacy and Social Studies Unit

Many teachers have experience weaving literacy and social studies units together to meet standards within each content area and to provide meaningful opportunities for students to read, to write, and to understand our world. These units can be beautiful places to center Black histories through the use of children's books that explore history and strengthen literacy skills.

The Social Studies Component of *Unspeakable*

During our kindergarten social studies history unit, "Then and Now," I used the book *Unspeakable: The Tulsa Race Massacre*, written by Carole Boston Weatherford and illustrated by Floyd Cooper, which centers a Black historical moment outside of the Civil Rights Movement and slavery (the parts of Black history that are given most focus in school, often to the neglect of all other moments and eras of Black history). Our Missouri social studies standards ask elementary students to understand "continuity and change in the history of Missouri and the United States" (Missouri Department of Elementary and Secondary Education 2016, 5). Many states have a similar standard that focuses on change and continuity in state and U.S. history. In kindergarten, students' activities in our "Then and Now" unit often include creating personal histories (timelines) of their lives and comparing their family's life in the past and the present.

At the same time that we study the past and present in social studies, my students are also learning to retell key details in a story; identify story elements such as the characters, setting, and plot; and recognize parts of a book.

Timelines and even the understanding of the passage of time are sometimes challenging for young children, so before we jump into creating personal histories, I introduced timelines and how events unfold over time through *Unspeakable*. The book tells the story of the Tulsa Race Massacre of 1921 in which white Tulsans attacked and destroyed the thriving Black community in the Greenwood district of Tulsa, Oklahoma. As explained in the book flap that introduces the book, "Celebrated author Carole Boston Weatherford and acclaimed illustrator Floyd Cooper provide a sensitive and powerful introduction to the Tulsa Race Massacre, helping young readers understand the events of the past so we can move toward a better future for all" (Weatherford 2021).

Unspeakable was not specifically listed as a resource in my district's unit, but I knew that the book's connection with the broader focuses of the standard—historical perspective, historical thinking, and the passage of time—made this book a perfect choice for this unit.

The Read-Aloud Experience with *Unspeakable*

Since beginning to use *Unspeakable* in my classroom, I've read the book with two different classes. The first group of kindergarteners had a lot to say during the read-aloud. They wanted to know what was going to happen next, they wanted to point out observations from the illustrations, and they wanted to question parts of the text they didn't quite understand. The second group of kindergartners I read it to were quiet during the entire read-aloud. No one asked questions, no one pointed out observations from the illustrations, and few initially seemed eager to join in a discussion of the story.

Knowing that children (just like adults) may need time to process the book and a part of Black history with which they were unfamiliar, I gave my students that time. After reading the book, I grabbed a stack of blank paper and gave one piece to each student. I asked them to go back to their tables and write about any thoughts and feelings they had about what we read. As the children began to work, the room was quiet except for the music we play in the background during work time. Five minutes into their drawing and writing time, I began hearing chatter from the tables. I left my desk and went to check in with each table. I asked each group whether I could sit down, and once they agreed, I joined them and listened to their conversations.

"I drew a line down the middle of my paper," Caroline shared with her table group.

"I folded mine," Virna added.

"Yeah. I split the paper like the town. Black people on one side. White people on the other side." Duaa showed me.

"Look at my fire. There was fire, and they wouldn't put it out," Hassan shared.

These conversations went on for another five minutes as the students processed the events depicted in the book before we all gathered back on the carpet to share what we wrote about. I could have easily collected their papers and moved on to the next lesson, but the conversations students had at their tables showed me they were ready to process this book together through discussion, and their comments about the segregation of the town and the fire that occurred were at the center. It was important to me that they could talk about the key details, but I wanted to ensure that they knew what led up to those events. I thought that by meeting as a whole group and retelling other details from the text, we could identify the events leading up to the fire.

The next day, we gathered on the carpet and I asked, "Can y'all tell me what you remember from the book yesterday? I know there was a fire and the Black and white people were separated, but what else happened?" Again, I wanted to see what other information they had gathered from the book while also validating what they had written about and discussed at their tables the day before. After I looked at the list we created (Figure 3.4), I noticed that quite a bit of the text had stuck with them. Even though they weren't as vocal during the read-aloud, their quietness did not mean they did not understand the content.

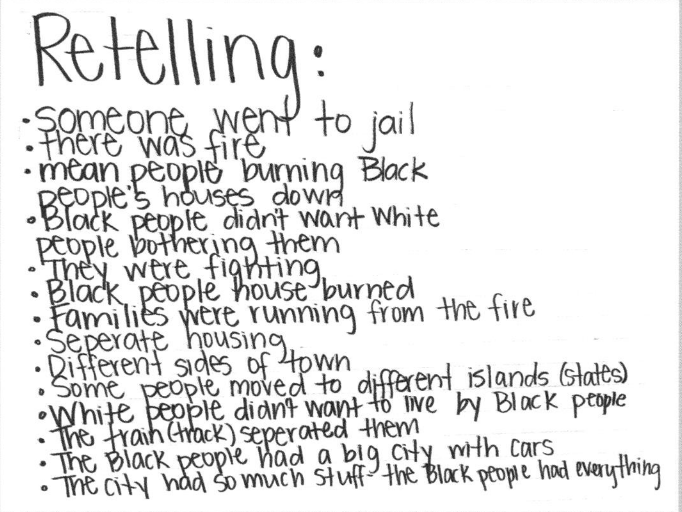

I took this work a step further and brought in story maps. Using key details to retell stories and identifying

Retelling:
- someone went to jail
- there was fire
- mean people burning Black people's houses down
- Black people didn't want white people bothering them
- They were fighting
- Black people house burned
- families were running from the fire
- Seperate housing
- Different sides of town
- Some people moved to different islands (States)
- White people didn't want to live by Black people
- the train (track) seperated them
- The Black people had a big city with cars
- The city had so much stuff the Black people had everything

FIGURE 3.4. On our second day working with the book *Unspeakable,* the class retold and charted important events it depicted.

characters, setting, and major events in a story are two kindergarten language arts standards. I knew that introducing a story map would not only support students in meeting the standard but also help them process the book and this event in Black history. Flipping back through the pages of *Unspeakable*, we worked collaboratively as a class to use words and drawings to fill in the Setting and Characters panels in the story map. Independently, students worked on the Beginning, Middle, and End panels. The time we spent orally retelling the story together as a class and revisiting the pages of the book together over several days prepared them for engaging in this work on their own (Figure 3.5).

To wrap up our activities for this book, we integrated art by "re-creating" Greenwood as it was before the destruction (Figure 3.6). Although the story tells of a tragedy, I wanted my students to also remember what Greenwood was—its beauty and the success of the African Americans who lived, worked,

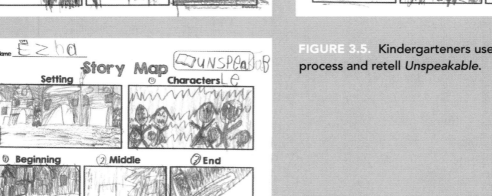

FIGURE 3.5. Kindergarteners used story maps to process and retell *Unspeakable*.

and built a community there. Despite the tremendous tragedy of the Tulsa Race Massacre, some Greenwood residents stayed to rebuild and keep the area alive. Even when we are teaching about tragedy, it is always important to emphasize change, resilience, and beauty.

When asked, "After what happened in Greenwood, would you stay or leave?" Sawyer answered, "I would stay and fix it."

Even though *Unspeakable* was not a resource referenced by my curriculum, I knew that bringing in this Black history and this particular book would help my students gain a deeper understanding of both our social studies focuses (historical perspective, historical thinking, and the passage of time) and our literacy focuses (recognizing key details, identifying story elements, and retelling a story).

I share this story of teaching literacy and social studies through the Black history in *Unspeakable* as one example

FIGURE 3.6. After reading *Unspeakable*, students made cut-paper art to show the beauty of Greenwood.

of the ways you can connect to and go beyond your existing curriculum. We cannot wait for standards and curricular materials to share and center Black histories—we must find ways of doing this work in our classrooms now.

Whether you use *Unspeakable* or another Black history–focused resource, you can adapt the same process for adding to, revising, challenging, and disrupting the curriculum. And you can do this while also meeting required standards and goals. Begin by understanding your standards and curricular resources across content areas. Then consider how you might connect this work to a part of Black history you'd like to highlight.

Who We Are as Readers and Writers: Representation in Literacy Units

Many teachers begin the school year with literacy units that help students explore the work of readers and writers. These early-in-the-school-year reading units might include an exploration of how readers choose books and how readers talk about books, as well as discussion of classroom community expectations for reading time. For writing, children might begin by telling oral stories, learning about different kinds of writing, and trying out different writing and illustration craft moves they notice in picture books.

As we cocreate classroom communities of readers and writers, it is important that we show diverse representations of readers and writers in the world. Often when we look for representations of readers and writers in picture books, we are presented with illustrations of white children. It is our job to give students a fuller and more representative image of what it means to be a reader and writer in the world, and one way we can do that is by selecting mentor texts to help us.

As we choose mentor texts for a variety of purposes—whether to study such craft moves as the use of specific adjectives to describe settings and characters, or simply to study what it means to be a reader and a writer in and beyond the classroom—we can search out books with characters who showcase Black brilliance. Here are a few of my favorite picture books that center Black children in their identities as readers and writers.

TEACHER TIP

You can use many different texts to achieve goals similar to those discussed in this section. Another favorite picture book of mine is *We Shall Overcome* by Bryan Collier. This book celebrates the popular civil rights protest and gospel song while encouraging readers to connect to both the past and the present. Seeing the past and present collide on the page helps students visualize the history.

Abdul's Story, written by Jamilah Thompkins-Bigelow and illustrated by Tiffany Rose

Abdul loves to tell stories, but struggles with writing in school until a visiting writer comes to his class and helps Abdul realize that making mistakes is a part of writing and that his stories are important to tell.

My Very Favorite Book in the Whole Wide World, written by Malcolm Mitchell and illustrated by Michael Robertson

Henley is a boy with a lot of interests, but reading just isn't one of them. What will he do when he gets a school assignment to bring in his favorite book to share with the class? This book explores what it means to be a reader and includes a note from author Malcolm Mitchell about his own journey as a reader.

How to Read a Book, written by Kwame Alexander and illustrated by Melissa Sweet

A poem in the form of a picture book, *How to Read a Book* invites readers into the sensory experience of what it means to be a reader.

Octopus Stew by Eric Velasquez

This picture book celebrates the power of oral storytelling, bilingualism, and imagination as it weaves the story of Ramsey, Grandma, and octopus stew. Written and illustrated by Afro-Latino author Eric Velasquez, the book even includes a recipe for pulpo guisado from the author's dad.

Woke: A Young Poet's Call to Justice, written by Mahogany L. Browne with Elizabeth Acevedo and Olivia Gatwood and illustrated by Theodore Taylor III

This collection of poems explores social justice and activism and encourages readers and writers to use their words as a way to speak up for those whose voices have been silenced.

Milo Imagines the World, written by Matt de la Peña and illustrated by Christian Robinson

While riding the subway with his sister, Milo imagines and reimagines the world around him through illustrations in his notebook. He learns that we cannot always imagine the lives of people solely based on what they look like.

As author Derrick Barnes said, "I think it's so important—for not only Black children—it's important for white children to see Black children as lead characters" (2022). Regardless of which standards or curriculum we use, we can all take a critical step toward more inclusive teaching by choosing picture books that illustrate readers and writers as diverse groups of people.

Centering Black Brilliance Within Science Units

Science was one of my least favorite subjects in school. I found it to be quite boring except for that time we dissected a sheep's eye in seventh grade. In elementary school, I remember science being done in a workbook and consisting of memorizing terms and their definitions. Because I did not have the best experience with science in school, I wanted my students to have a different experience than I did, but I was not sure how I was going to engage my students enough for them to enjoy it.

Black Scientists to Read About

These books introduce students to Black scientists and the work they do in their fields. These books are great models for students to see scientific processes in action as well as the paths these scientists took to develop their ideas and inventions we use today.

Buzzing with Questions: The Inquisitive Mind of Charles Henry Turner, written by Janice N. Harrington and illustrated by Theodore Taylor III

The Secret Garden of George Washington Carver, written by Gene Barretta and illustrated by Frank Morrison

Whoosh! Lonnie Johnson's Super-Soaking Stream of Inventions, written by Chris Barton and illustrated by Don Tate

Patricia's Vision: The Doctor Who Saved Sight, written by Michelle Lord and illustrated by Alleanna Harris

When you type "famous scientists" into a Google search, nine scientists and their pictures display on the results page: Albert Einstein, Isaac Newton, Thomas Edison, Galileo Galilei, Nicolaus Copernicus, Michael Faraday, Archimedes, and Marie Curie—eight white men and one white woman. I learned about quite a few of these scientists when I was in school, and they made some great contributions to science, but they weren't the only ones who did. Some people are missing, wouldn't you agree?

Before my students and I dive into our first science topic of the school year, I pose the question, "What does a scientist look like?" I give my students a sheet of paper and tell them to draw their idea. Quite often, they draw a white man, in a white lab coat, with large hair and beakers in his hands. That was my image of what a scientist looked like when I was in school too! Because that's what I was taught. Almost all the scientists I learned about in school were old (or dead!) white men with white hair. And even though a good amount of time has passed since I was a student learning science in school, many of my students still have this same image in their minds.

Scientists to Follow Online

Social media can be a great place to see what's currently going on in the world of science and to view photos of scientists at work in the field.

* Earyn McGee (herpetologist): @Afro_Herper (Twitter and Instagram)

* Raven Baxter (molecular biologist): @ravenscimave (Twitter) @raventhesciencemaven (Instagram)

* Neil deGrasse Tyson (astrophysicist): @neiltyson (Twitter) @neildegrassetyson (Instagram)

* Mae C. Jemison (engineer): @maejemison (Twitter)

Oftentimes, children are taught about the oppression and racism within Black history, rather than the brilliance and intelligence of Black people. Science is one avenue for introducing students to the innovation and ingenuity present throughout Black history and how it impacts us currently. It is also a great opportunity to acknowledge the Black people who are currently contributing to science.

Adding to the Curriculum with Ernest Everett Just

"Someone who researches and learns about living things is called a biologist," I announce to my class one morning.

"We are biologists?" Alex asks.

"We are learning about living things, and they need food, water, and air," Anderson chimes in.

"And shelter!" Bruce adds.

"You biologists remembered a lot of information!" I comment. "Today I am going to read a true story about another biologist and the living things he studied."

Ernest Everett Just was a teacher and a biologist who studied marine worms. His mom taught him how to read, his dad died when he was just four years old, and he studied biology in both the United States and France. This information comes from several lists of facts my kindergartners created using the template I created (Figure 3.7) after we read *The Vast Wonder of the World: Biologist Ernest Everett Just*, written by Mélina Mangal and illustrated by Luisa Uribe.

One of my state's science standards for kindergartners is to make observations in order to describe what plants and animals need to survive. This work includes identifying plants and animals, categorizing what a need is and what a want is, and recognizing what it is that organisms need in order to survive.

One way I make science come alive for my students is by introducing them to Black scientists such as Ernest Everett Just and George Washington Carver, who contributed to the fields of biology and botany and offer us a window into how scientists (presently and throughout history) ask and investigate questions. We follow up these studies of scientists and their work by engaging in our own scientific inquiry—for example, growing plants as Carver did or looking at cells under a microscope as Just did.

Ernest Everett Just helped me bring science alive for my students through an integration of history and

FIGURE 3.7. A template I made in PowerPoint for my students to use as they created their list of facts about Ernest Everett Just

literacy. He helped add to my students' understanding of living things by introducing them to marine organisms we cannot see with our naked eye. Learning about Just's science stirred their curiosity by nudging their understanding of what a living organism can look like. Learning about Just's life supports students' inquiry about the world around them and provides another image of what a scientist can look like.

More Black Scientists to Learn About

These Black scientists (and many, many more) have contributed a great deal to their fields. These are a few scientists whose work might align with topics within the elementary curriculum:

* Benjamin Banneker (naturalist, mathematician astronomer)
* George Robert Caruthers (physicist, engineer, space scientist)
* Mary Maynard Daly (biochemist)
* Annie Easley (rocket scientist)
* Percy L. Julian (chemist)
* Wangari Maathai (environmentalist)
* Charles Henry Turner (zoologist)
* Warren M. Washington (atmospheric scientist)

Remembering That Black Scientists Exist

Ernest Everett Just is just one of many Black scientists who have made contributions to the world of science. There are plenty of other opportunities to connect the life sciences with books by Black authors and with Black characters. Many books about science, gardens, and the natural world feature white scientists and white characters. By contrast, books such as *Harlem Grown: How One Big Idea Transformed a Neighborhood*, written by Tony Hillery and illustrated by Jessie Hartland, and *The Thing About Bees: A Love Letter by Shabazz Larkin* are great for encouraging children to honor their environment and the organisms that live there through reading about Black characters as caretakers of and experts on the world around them.

Uncover the Curriculum

I strive to teach the history many rarely are taught in schools.

—Leo Glazé, history educator

Recently I was talking with some colleagues, and we were discussing how Black history is often kept hidden behind a thick curtain. Some educators keep the curtain closed. They know Black history is there, but they are going to teach what they are "supposed to" teach, what is explicitly named in the curriculum and standards. Other educators peek behind the curtain from time to time, choosing what they will and won't teach. Some educators completely ignore the curtain and everything behind it because they refuse to teach Black histories. But then there are those of us who choose to keep the curtain open and see the possibilities that Black histories offer our classrooms. Whether through science or math or social studies or language arts, there is room for Black histories; whether Black histories are incorporated throughout an entire unit or simply a focus for the week, we understand that they embody knowledge and truth that can't be taught in one month.

Beyond the Month

4

By 1921 over 80 percent of black high schools celebrated Negro History Week—an educational initiative he [Carter G. Woodson] created in 1926, which later became Black History Month in 1976. Negro History Week was also widely celebrated in elementary schools and popularly covered in the black press around the country.

—Jarvis R. Givens, *Fugitive Pedagogy: Carter G. Woodson and the Art of Black Teaching* (2021, 17)

Carter G. Woodson is often referred to as the Father of Black History. He was a historian, teacher, and journalist who studied the history of African Americans. Woodson, alongside the Association for the Study of Negro Life and History, which he founded in 1915, launched Negro History Week in 1926. Negro History Week, which was initially celebrated during the second week of February to coincide with the birthdays of Frederick Douglass and Abraham Lincoln, was designed as time to celebrate and study the history of African Americans in the United States. While the creation of Negro History Week was met with both enthusiasm and resistance from different groups of people and organizations, from the very beginning an important emphasis of the week was the teaching and learning of Black history in public schools.

The first Black History Month was celebrated in 1970 by Black students and educators at Kent State University. Six years later, President Gerald Ford recognized Black History Month at the United States Bicentennial in 1976.

The origins of Negro History Week and Black History Month are deeply rooted in schools and the work of teachers and students. Yet the purpose of both Negro History Week and Black History Month has never been to cram the history of an entire group of people into a single short time period; it is not a time for students to be *introduced* to Black history. Black History Month should be a time for students and teachers to showcase what they have learned all year and to celebrate the diverse Black histories of our country.

Don't wait until February to pull out those Black History Month book collections and activities. When we teach Black history throughout the year, Black History Month can be exactly what Carter G. Woodson intended it to be: a *celebration* and *extension* of the histories.

Getting Started with Black History Month

When I was in elementary school, I knew that February was Black History Month, but it wasn't celebrated at my school. We learned about Martin Luther King Jr. around his birthday in January, but Valentine's Day is what dominated February in school.

Now, every year, as a teacher, I stay after school the day before the first day of February and set up for Black History Month. I print out pictures, make signs, bring in artifacts, check out books from the library, and plan what I am going to do with my students each day in February. I hang photos from the ceiling and create a massive book display with books that center Black people, history, and culture.

But this isn't what my first Black History Month celebration looked like . That first year, I had a small brown bookshelf, a picture frame, and a few books (Figure 4.1). Each day I changed out the picture in the frame to display a different Black historical figure, and I read a book focused on that person during our morning meeting. As the years went on and I began to better understand the purpose and history of Black History Month, my celebration grew. It wasn't until I further educated myself that I began to develop Black History Month themes, activities, and experiences that my students could learn from, while also integrating the Black history we had studied throughout the year.

You might start with a little bookshelf this school year, a special place to highlight important figures in Black history through photos, books, and artifacts. Or you might dig into creating a bigger, multifaceted celebration. Wherever you start, know that as you learn and grow as a Black history educator, so too can your celebration of Black History Month.

Some Favorite Ways to Celebrate Black History Month

When we study Black history throughout the year, February becomes a time in which we can focus on celebration and continued learning. We might choose to celebrate Black history through a study of African American cuisine, music, art, or any number of other Black histories. The next sections describe a few of my

FIGURE 4.1. My small brown bookshelf from my first year celebrating Black History Month as a teacher. On this day, a photo of Madam C. J. Walker is in the frame surrounded by hair grease, plastic rollers, and two hot combs. I brought these artifacts in to represent her work with hair care products for Black women. Although Walker popularized the use of the hot comb, this technology had existed since the 1870s (Bundles 2002). The shelves below display other Black history–focused books from my early collection.

favorite ways to celebrate Black History Month as one part of our continuous, yearlong, lifelong study of Black history.

Celebration Idea 1: Eat, Drink, and Celebrate African American Cuisine!

*We can be proud of classic casseroles that express **ingenuity** with repurposed leftovers, not just filling ourselves with scraps. And we're eager to hand down Grandmother's scratch-cooking recipes to our children.*

—Toni Tipton-Martin, *Jubilee: Recipes from Two Centuries of African American Cooking* (2019, 17)

Black history can be celebrated through many avenues, in many ways, and by many people. My family and I celebrate Black History Month by cooking food and making recipes that have been passed down from previous generations (Figure 4.2). I have used food as part of the Black History Month celebration in my classroom as well. Sometimes I share recipes with my students and ask families to send in pictures if they decide to make the recipe at home. I recently recorded one of my grandmothers making hot water cornbread and have shared that video with students. They come away from watching the video with a lot of questions, which leads us into further research. They want to learn the recipe, and I love sharing with them that my grandma keeps it a secret (she truly does!), but that she makes different batches of the cornbread, including a batch with jalapeño peppers.

FIGURE 4.2. For years I would end our class's Black History Month celebrations by bringing in banana pudding and sharing with students my family history with this dessert. I let them in on the secret that my family has two different banana pudding recipes—the real one and the lazy one.

"What does it taste like, Ms. James?" I am often asked.

I always respond with, "It is crunchy on the outside, with a warm and soft inside. I really like the spicy ones."

If you focus on cuisine during Black History Month, cookbooks are wonderful resources. Recipes tell stories. Although I don't have my grandmother's recipe, we can look to books such as *Jubilee: Recipes from Two Centuries of African American Cooking* by Toni Tipton-Martin to explore a hot water cornbread recipe and read about the different shapes and sizes of cornbread. We can also learn about how history intersects with food in cookbooks such as Nicole A. Taylor's (2022) *Watermelon and Red Birds: A Cookbook for Juneteenth and Black Celebrations*, which tells some of the history of the Atlanta Student Movement. The stories within these recipes and cookbooks can spark our students' curiosity about the stories their own family recipes tell. It is important for children to see many kinds of texts and learn about the different places they can gather information as researchers and young historians. In addition, cookbooks provide excellent opportunities for students to engage with real-world mathematics. As you add recipes and cookbooks to your classroom library, students will begin to value and cherish these resources.

The Food Finds Learning Lab from the National Museum of African American History and Culture

Discussing the history of African American cuisine, sharing recipes, and bringing in banana pudding and my grandma's sweet potato pie have been a way not only to celebrate but to share Black history in my classroom. It is also important to emphasize that there isn't just *one* kind of Black or even African American cuisine. A study of Black cooking reflects Black ingenuity and brilliance just as a study of Black inventors or Black scientists does. As Toni Tipton-Martin writes in *Jubilee,* "Whether cooks adapted kosher dishes in Jewish homes across the South, mingled with Cuban and Puerto Rican immigrants in Harlem, or experimented with Mexican ingredients in the West, a beautiful cuisine blossomed" (2019, 16). Learning these histories can help you and your students celebrate food in a new way.

Check out these food enthusiasts on Instagram and grow your teacher knowledge:

* Tabitha Brown (@iamtabithabrown)
* Gabrielle Eitienne (@gabriell_eitienne)
* Stephen Satterfield (@isawstephen)
* Nicole Taylor (@foodculturist)
* Michael W. Twitty (@thecookinggene)

I would also suggest checking out the National Museum of African American History and Culture's Learning Lab. The lab's "Food Finds: Food Objects in the NMAAHC Collection" is a great resource for viewing artifacts such as photographs, dishes, and recipes that also tell stories of food and culture within Black history.

Celebration Idea 2: Choose a Theme for Black History Month

One way to celebrate Black History Month is to choose a theme or focus that highlights an element of Black culture, joy, agency, or history. I begin this work each year by curating a collection of books about a theme or topic. As you may remember from earlier chapters, one of my favorite Black history themes is inventors and inventions (Figure 4.3). With this theme, we spend the month using picture books, photos, blueprints, and other artifacts to explore the history of Black inventors and inventions and highlight Black ingenuity and brilliance. If you choose this focus, you can refer back to the book collection about inventors and inventions described Chapter 2.

FIGURE 4.3. After our celebration of African American inventors, students in my class made short videos using FlipGrid to share about their favorite inventors. QR codes for these videos were displayed outside our classroom during family/teacher conferences and the month of March. I also sent home each student's QR code so their families could see their videos. These videos became a major talking point during family/teacher conferences because parents were so proud of their child and eager to share this QR code with other family members and friends.

Each time I celebrate Black History Month with the theme of inventors and inventions, it looks a little different. For example, one year I focused on hair-related inventions. We learned about Madam C. J. Walker, I asked students to bring in hair products they use, and I created a book collection about hair.

Another year when I taught in a multiage classroom, we studied a different inventor or invention each day. I had a table dedicated to this project, and each morning, when students came in, there would be a clue, riddle, or multiple-choice question for them to engage with in order to figure out who the inventor of the day was. That particular year, I hung four banners from the ceiling that displayed information about different Black inventors and their inventions. Children used these banners as a text and resource for figuring out who the inventor of the day was.

Yet another year, my coteacher and I celebrated hidden figures in Black history (Figure 4.4). Each day in February, one of us would wear a name tag with a hidden figure's name on it. Our students would ask us who we were, and we would introduce ourselves as that person, telling about that person's life and contributions.

Yet another year, I created a photo gallery of images from different Black histories. There were flags from different African countries, quotes from

FIGURE 4.4 This photo was taken during our "Hidden Figures Within Black History" year. I gave each of my students a party hat and painted a poster that said, "Happy Black History Month!" I wanted my students not only to *know* we were celebrating but also to *look* and **feel** like we were celebrating. Behind me you can see a sign that reads, "WALK a mile in their shoes." After learning about a different "hidden figure" each day, on the outline of a shoe we would write one fact about the person we read about and hang it up to remember whom we had talked about and think about their perspectives.

Malcolm X, snapshots of Michael Jordan, newspaper articles, and other photos that captured moments in Black history. There was no theme that year, so my students decided to name it "A Gallery Walk Through Black History," and each day they chose an image from the gallery about which to learn (Figure 4.5). The element of student choice enabled us to focus on the intersection of students' interests and Black history.

Whatever theme for a Black History Month celebration you choose, know that you do not need to be an expert to get started. Take Black History Month as an opportunity to engage in inquiry alongside your students and model what it means to be a curious lifelong learner.

A Few Ideas for Black History Month Themes

* Sports
* Leaders
* Cowboys
* Cuisines
* Art
* Joy

* Africa
* Architects
* Music
* Dance
* Poetry
* Local Black histories

FIGURE 4.5. This photo was taken on the first day of one of our Black History Month celebrations. This was the year of "A Gallery Walk Through Black History," and we focused on many Black histories instead of just one. Each year for Black History Month I buy a T-shirt that centers Black history. I actually used the words on this T-shirt for an activity!

Celebration Idea 3: Share a Love of Black Music

Music is a wonderful way to bring Black histories into the classroom. Using songs of protest, spirituals, and hip hop, my students have analyzed lyrics and discussed the ways that different songs convey messages about strength, power, encouragement, comfort, and support. "Freedom" by Bebe's Kids and Tone Loc, "My Power" by Beyoncé, "Baldwin" by Jamila Woods, and "Glory" by John Legend and Common are just a few of many songs I have brought into the classroom to celebrate Black history and analyze the message each song brings. You might choose music from a particular time period you are studying, current music, or a mix of the two. Working with songs as short texts can be a powerful way to sprinkle in a celebration of Black history throughout the day.

Celebration Idea 4: Create Black History Stations to Give Kids Hands-on Experiences

Stations are a great way to give students some choice to explore topics that are interesting to them. I often do stations first thing in the morning after Morning Meeting or during our literacy time, but you could create stations that align with the goals of any part of your day. If you are celebrating Black History Month with a theme, your stations can center on that theme, or they can just be an eclectic mix. You can have students choose from different stations, or you can have all the students doing the same activity, just in table groups around the room instead of as the whole group.

TEACHER TIP

Curate a playlist of music by Black artists. Your playlist might have a theme, such as music from a certain time period or a type of music, or it might be an eclectic mix of your and your students' favorites.

Here's a playlist I love to share with students:

* The Message —Grandmaster Flash
* U.N.I.T.Y.—Queen Latifah
* Say It Loud—James Brown
* The Revolution Will Not Be Televised—Gil Scott-Heron
* A Change Is Gonna Come —Sam Cooke
* What's Going On —Marvin Gaye
* Living for the City —Stevie Wonder
* Black Man—Stevie Wonder
* Guarding the Gates —Lauryn Hill
* K.R.I.T. Here—Big K.R.I.T.

The options for stations are endless! Here are a few of my favorite station ideas that I have created over the years:

* **Hair and Black culture station**

  Students watch a short video about hair in Black culture and then use a black strip of paper (representing a strand of hair) and a white crayon to write down a fact or idea that they learned from the video (Figure 4.6). Once students have created their strands, roll the papers into curls and add them to a classroom door or hallway decoration (Figure 4.7).

* **Inventor and invention matching game station**

  Students work together to match the inventor with their invention (Figure 4.8). You could use this same matching game idea with any Black history topic your class has explored, such as Black scientists and their contributions or Black artists and their artwork.

* ***Black Panther* station**

  The year the movie *Black Panther* was released in theaters, my class designed our own Black Panther masks and learned about the costume designer on the movie, Ruth Carter.

* **Black history book exploration stations**

  One of the simplest stations to set up is a book exploration station at which students can explore books about a single topic or a variety of topics in Black history.

FIGURE 4.6. After watching a short video about hair in Black culture, students wrote facts on black construction paper representing hair. We used the "hair" to create a door decoration in celebration of Black History Month (Figure 4.7).

FIGURE 4.7. A student poses next to our classroom door display celebrating Black hair that she and her classmates helped create.

* **Music station**

  You can set up a station at which students can listen to songs by Black artists and draw in response to how the song makes them feel. Consider printing off lyrics with which students can follow along as they listen to the songs.

* **Artifact exploration station**

  My favorite station to set up is an artifact exploration. I love bringing in artifacts that support an understanding of Black history and give students an opportunity to engage in a hands-on way. You might bring in artifacts all related to a particular idea, time period, or theme in Black history. For example, when we talk about Madam C. J. Walker or read books about hair by Sharee Miller, I bring in a hot comb. I tell my students stories about what the hot comb is used for and how my aunties used it to straighten my hair. Students always make the connection that it is similar to the hair straightener their mom or sister might use.

FIGURE 4.8. Students match photos of Black inventors to their inventions.

Celebration Idea 5: Invite a Guest Speaker to Visit Your Classroom in Person or Virtually

Guest speakers are a great way to bring Black history to life. David Brown is a Paralympian for Team USA and is the fastest completely blind man in the world. His mom and my dad worked together, so it was only right that I inquired about having him talk to my class. We spent some time learning about Brown the week of his visit and watched a video of one of his races. We created a list of questions that we wanted to ask him, and my students took turns asking them during a FaceTime call. Years later, those students still talk about when we were on FaceTime with David Brown. Reach out to Black authors, illustrators, leaders, musicians, or entrepreneurs and invite them

TEACHER TIP

Use Black History Month as a time of continued self-education. For example, it wasn't until I went to the National Museum of African American History and Culture that I learned that Garrett Morgan, inventor of the gas mask and the traffic light, is also responsible for inventing the first straightening comb with curved teeth. As a lifetime student of Black history, I am always learning and sharing my learning with my students.

into your classrooms. Twitter and Instagram are great platforms for connecting with people, and, in my experience, many are eager for the opportunity to talk with young people. Also consider inviting guest speakers during months other than February—we want to convey both to our students *and* to our guest speakers that Black history and expertise are valuable all year long.

Take Note

When you are teaching Black histories year round, you'll notice which topics your students respond to and what their interests are. Bring that information into your Black History Month celebrations. One year I had a class of dancers; they danced to any and everything—even the school bell. I brought their love for dance into Black History Month with such books as *When the Beat Was Born*, written by Laban Carrick Hill and illustrated by Theodore Taylor III, and *The Roots of Rap*, written by Carole Boston Weatherford and illustrated by Frank Morrison; by showing music videos such as "Jump" by Kriss Kross; and by giving them space to dance along with dance performances. Another year, I had a class of artists who enjoyed painting, drawing, and creating clay sculptures. Black History Month that year was a time to celebrate their skills and the lives of Black artists such as Alma Thomas, Augusta Savage, and Jean-Michel Basquiat. The best teaching is responsive to the students in front of us, and the teaching of Black history and celebrating of Black History Month should be no different!

Whether you decorate your classroom door, create a book display, cook a dish from African American cuisine, curate a classroom playlist, or have a small brown shelf with a few books and a picture frame, use February as a moment of celebration. A moment to further engage with the Black history that has been in your classroom throughout the year. And a moment to recognize and highlight Black joy and community—past, present, and future.

The Work Doesn't Stop Here

5

If we intend to teach accurate history and empower our students to walk through our nation and the world wide awake, we must become racially conscious ourselves and relentlessly pursue the truth.

—Aeriale Johnson (2021, 5)

Think of this book as a starting point. It cannot answer *all* your questions about ways to integrate Black history into your curriculum. This book cannot plan out *every* conversation you will have with students about race. This book cannot give you a list of *every* great children's book that centers Black histories. What this book *can* do is share with you *some* ways that Black joy can be alive throughout the year in your classroom. What this book *can* do is show you ways in which all children, not just Black children, benefit from the learning of Black histories. What this book *can* do is support your continued work of teaching through these Black histories in your classroom.

I want to leave you with some things to remember:

* Educate yourself and do the research first. But don't let fear of not knowing everything or making a mistake stop you from introducing Black histories into your classroom. You will not know the answer to every question students ask. You may make mistakes. But if you position yourself as a lifelong learner of Black histories, you can do this work.

* Start with Black innovation, joy, and pride. American slavery should not be children's first introduction to Black history. ·

* Go beyond the Civil Rights Movement. The Civil Rights Movement is an important part of Black history, but not the only part. There are many other Black histories before, during, and after the Civil Rights Movement.

* Look for Black people throughout world history; they are there! African American history isn't the only Black history.

* Make space, room, and time for Black people, their histories, presents, and futures in curricula.

* Understand that no Black history is too hard for children to learn. There are developmentally appropriate ways of teaching all kinds of history.

I am constantly learning. Whether through reading books, watching documentaries, having conversations, or researching, I am always learning something new about Black histories. There are always new books being published, films being created, and research being done to support these histories and bring them to the forefront. Once you begin to apply a lens of Black history to your teaching, the ways you view your curriculum, and your own learning, you can't help but want to keep discovering, learning, and unlearning. Just as scientists never proclaim themselves to be "done" or "finished" learning all the science there is to know or understanding how the world works, we will never be finished with our learning of Black histories.

I hope that throughout your journey with this book, you see that Black history cannot be crammed into February, and it shouldn't have to be. Shift, shake, cut, or do whatever you must to make room in your classrooms for the Black histories that fill the world with genius, perseverance, joy, and truth.

FREQUENTLY ASKED QUESTIONS ABOUT BLACK HISTORY EDUCATION

After presentations, webinars, and workshops, I often receive a variety of questions about teaching Black history. In this section, I answer some of the frequently asked questions I receive from educators. Of course, these are my experiences, opinions, advice, and thoughts—someone else might respond differently! The important thing is to keep learning from others' work, from research you do, and from your experiences teaching through a Black history lens.

Q What should I do if I receive pushback from school administrators, families, community members, or colleagues about centering Black histories in my teaching?

A It is undeniable that we teach in a time when simply teaching historical truth or reading students picture books that feature children of color is viewed by some as "indoctrination," "too political," or "not appropriate for children." Educators may rightly worry that teaching Black history carries risk. *What if parents complain? What if my principal doesn't support me? What if a book I cherish is restricted or banned in my district?* There is no doubt that teaching truth often requires bravery and is never risk free. My best advice is to teach Black history honestly, transparently, and boldly.

As you engage in teaching Black history, it is important, for multiple reasons, that you are knowledgeable about your state's standards and your school or district's curricula. Finding ways to consistently and transparently view your standards and curricula through a Black history lens is one way to increase the likelihood that what you do will be valued and understood by those outside the classroom. I have never taught anything in my classroom that did not align, in some way, with my state's learning standards. As I plan units, I always make sure that the connections I make between Black history and the standards are transparent both to families and to school and district colleagues.

This transparency and honesty with my students' families is critical. I never hide anything! And why should I? We proudly hang up our work both inside and outside the classroom for all to see. I also collaborate with other teachers in my school, and share lessons and activities from in my classroom on social media. I take any opportunity to share my students' art and writing with

FREQUENTLY ASKED QUESTIONS ABOUT BLACK HISTORY EDUCATION

families, sending home video clips, sharing documentation of students' work during family/teacher conferences, and sending home newsletters that describe class activities. Most families are overwhelmingly supportive of the work we do when they have opportunities to ask questions and celebrate their children's learning.

I also understand that there are places that have banned (or are trying to ban) teaching, reading, and talking about anything related to race. One thing my mama taught me, which I will share with you, is that when you get pushed, push back. Just as you would show evidence of how a student is meeting or not meeting a standard on a report card or at a family/teacher conference, show the evidence when it comes to teaching Black histories. Show evidence of how what you teach students aligns with your state standards and makes a difference in students' learning.

Only you know the environment in which you teach and how much push-back you may receive. You will ultimately have to make the decisions about which books to read and what parts of history to center. As you do so, I encourage you to do so with as much bravery, transparency, and boldness as you can. Remember why you are doing this work. When we experience fear or pushback, we can reflect on and center why we think teaching Black history is so critically important. And try to find spaces and people that will embrace your work and celebrate it alongside you!

Q Many of the picture books in *Beyond February* were new to me! How do you find out about amazing picture books for teaching Black history?

A Social media is a great place for learning about new and exciting children's books. I follow many accounts on Instagram, including those of my favorite authors and illustrators, book publishers, book reviewers, educators, and fellow lovers of children's books that center Black history. I also spend a lot of time in local bookstores browsing their children's book selections and flipping through the pages of new-to-me books for both children and adults.

FREQUENTLY ASKED QUESTIONS ABOUT BLACK HISTORY EDUCATION

If you're interested in learning about the latest and greatest picture books, I suggest following a few of my favorite book-celebrating Instagram pages:

Corrie (@thetinyactivists)
Eliana (@kidlitismagic)
Johanna & Lauren (@jojos_book_club)
Shannon Griffin (@literally_cultured)
Megan Reid (@ihaveabook4that)
Vera Ahiyya (@thetututeacher)

Q How do I teach Black history if my students are mostly or all white?

 Teach Black history as you would any other history—with purpose, accurate information, and high-quality resources. I too have taught in a space in which 95 percent of my students were white. That didn't stop me from teaching Black histories or change how I taught them. Most of the Black History Month celebrations mentioned in this book were celebrated with the students in that classroom. All students in our country need a full and robust understanding of American history, especially Black history. As Wintre Foxworth Johnson states, "by centering Black history, Black cultural production, and Black resistance, we create space for children to collectively and collaboratively make meaning about history and racial realities" (2022, 176).

Some people argue that teaching about race, racism, or parts of Black history makes white children "feel guilty." In fact, recent legislation restricting what teachers can talk about or the books they can read to students often relies on the argument that simply teaching truthful history or reading books about Black children is in some way traumatic to white children. But as Ursula Wolfe-Rocca and Christie Nold write in their article, "Why the Narrative That Critical Race Theory 'Makes White Kids Feel Guilty' Is a Lie," "Students are hungry for explanations—real explanations—for the world they have inherited, and in our experience, they often feel relieved to gain insight into why things are the way they are" (2022).

FREQUENTLY ASKED QUESTIONS ABOUT BLACK HISTORY EDUCATION

Black history education is not for one group of children. It is important that *all* children understand our country's history, including Black history. Moreover, many times the topics discussed in classrooms come from children's own questions about the world around them. And as Wolfe-Rocca and Nold assert in their article, teachers are experts at responding to children's questions and ideas in ways that are both accurate and developmentally appropriate. "Our curriculum emphasizes the varied, powerful and creative ways that people have resisted oppression and built justice. We are careful to offer students models of action, examples of people just like them who have tried to change the world and sometimes succeeded. No, our classrooms are not incubators of cynicism. They are brimming with curiosity, conversation and, yes, joy" (Wolfe-Rocca and Nold 2022). Don't underestimate the brilliance of children who come to your classrooms with ideas, questions, and knowledge.

 How can I, as a white teacher, teach Black history?

A I am not all the things that I teach. When I teach my students about Indigenous people, Hispanic heritage, LGBTQIA folx, or any other person or group of people who have different identities, cultures, or perspectives than my own, I have to research. I read books; I search websites; I ask questions; I center the voices of people who *do* identify as members of these communities. I enter into the work humbly with a commitment to continuous learning.

Like you, I want what I teach to be truthful and accurate. Of course, I *do* worry that I may say the wrong thing or make a mistake. And it's true that I am likely to make many mistakes along the way! But by committing to do the research and surround myself with others who can support me, I know I can help children in their lifelong journey of learning about the world around them, past and present.

"How Can White Teachers Teach Black History? Six Things You Need to Know" by Daniel P. Tulino, Greg Simmons, and Brianne R. Pitts

FREQUENTLY ASKED QUESTIONS ABOUT BLACK HISTORY EDUCATION

I am not white, so I suggest that if you are a white teacher, you check out the article cited here and other work and research from my colleagues and friends Dan Tulino, Greg Simmons, and Brianne Pitts, who have done research on white teachers teaching Black history. As these authors state, "White teachers must teach Black history. Not because we do it particularly well, but because nationally, we make up roughly 80 percent of the public K–12 workforce and we cannot rely on our colleagues of color to do this work for us. . . . In our experience, effectively teaching Black history requires white teachers like us to decenter our whiteness, address our fears, and develop a community of collaborators who will do this work alongside us" (Tulino, Simmons, and Pitts 2021).

Q How do I respond when people ask if I am teaching critical race theory (CRT)?

A CRT is a theory taught at the graduate level that addresses how race is constructed and embedded in institutions, systems, and laws. So no, teaching Black histories is not the same as CRT; it's social studies, math, science, literacy, and art.

In a Harvard EdCast podcast, Dr. Gloria Ladson-Billings, a professor emerita at the University of Wisconsin–Madison and the author of *Critical Race Theory in Education: A Scholar's Journey*, spoke about the erroneous labeling of truthful history teaching as critical race theory.

> What I find the most egregious about this situation is we are taking books out of classrooms, which is very anti-democratic. . . . And so you're saying that kids can't read the story of Ruby Bridges. It's okay for Ruby Bridges at six years old to have to have been escorted by federal marshals and have racial epithets spewed at her. It's just not okay for a six year old today to know that happened to her. I mean, one of the rationales for not talking about race, I don't even say critical race theory, but not talking about race in the classroom is we don't want white children to feel bad. (Anderson 2022)

FREQUENTLY ASKED QUESTIONS ABOUT BLACK HISTORY EDUCATION

Rather than spending time debating the use of the term *critical race theory*, we can better spend our energy planning for meaningful, truthful teaching.

Q　What do you do if learning Black history makes a student emotional?

A I cannot always predict how my students will react to the information shared or discussed in our classroom, but I do know that children experience a wide range of emotions as they learn about Black history. They may feel curious when they learn about Black scientists such as Ernest Everett Just. They may feel excited when we sample recipes from inventor and "father of ice cream" Augustus Jackson. They may feel sad or angry when we learn about segregation or slavery. They may feel inspired or proud when they learn about activists throughout Black history who took risks and fought for change. Feelings are OK! And I make sure that my teaching of Black history does not focus solely on tragedy and violence.

Any time a student does express feelings of sadness, anger, or confusion, I stop. I pause the activity, reading, or discussion. Oftentimes, other students will comfort those upset students and talk to them. Later I may pull that student aside and talk to them about how they are feeling. Young students are often honest with me about their feelings and what they are thinking. I comfort and reassure them that they are in a space where it is safe to express their feelings, and I am honest that I too experience anger and sadness about particular Black histories. I always contact the student's family to inform them of what I taught and what may have evoked emotion in their child. I also tell them about my one-on-one conversation with their child. I want to be fully transparent, just as if a student got hurt on the playground, so I give families as many of the details as I can. In my experience, the conversation continues at home, and families often communicate the outcome of that conversation with me.

Appendix

A Powerful People Set About _____

BIG IDEA: What do these people have in common? What makes them fit with the big idea of the set?

PEOPLE: Find three to five people who fit with the big idea of this set. List their names and dates of birth and death (if applicable).

JOB, CAREER, INVENTION, KNOWN FOR: This section will change depending on the big idea of the set. Be sure to list as much information as you can so as to avoid the danger of a repeated narrative.

DID YOU KNOW? As you research, what sticks out to you, and what might grab the attention of your students? What might be an important piece of information about the person that isn't well known or understood?

FOR MORE INFO: This is the space to list other resources for learning about the people in your set. These resources can include books, photographs, videos, interviews, songs, exhibits, and so on.

TRY THIS: As you're researching and exploring resources, think about an activity or task that will enable students to process and apply the information they're learning about the people in the set.

ALWAYS KEEP IN MIND . . . These Powerful People Sets cannot "cover" a person or a group of people's entire history. The information in these charts comprises only bits and pieces of the lives they lived, not their whole story. I challenge you to discover and learn more on your own and with your students. Use these charts as starting points, be careful of those repeated narratives, and remember to tell the truth, as fully as you can.

Children's Book References

Abdul-Jabbar, Kareem, with Raymond Obstfeld. 2013. *What Color Is My World? The Lost History of African-American Inventors*. Illustrated by Ben Boos and A. G. Ford. Somerville, MA: Candlewick.

Alexander, Kwame. 2019. *How to Read a Book*. Illustrated by Melissa Sweet. New York: HarperCollins.

Alexander, Kwame. 2019. *The Undefeated*. Illustrated by Kadir Nelson. New York: Versify.

Alexander, Kwame, with Chris Colderley and Marjory Wentworth. 2017. *Out of Wonder: Poems Celebrating Poets*. Illustrated by Ekua Holmes. Somerville, MA: Candlewick.

Allen, Tessa. 2020. *Sometimes People March*. New York: Balzer + Bray.

Angelou, Maya. 2018. *Life Doesn't Frighten Me*. Illustrated by Jean-Michel Basquiat. New York: Harry N. Abrams.

Armand, Glenda, and Kim Freeman. 2023. *Ice Cream Man: How Augustus Jackson Made a Sweet Treat Better*. Illustrated by Keith Mallett. New York: Crown Books for Young Readers.

Atinuke. 2019. *Africa, Amazing Africa: Country by Country*. Illustrated by Mouni Feddag. London: Walker Books.

Barnes, Derrick. 2017. *Crown: An Ode to the Fresh Cut*. Illustrated by Gordon C. James. Chicago: Agate Bolden.

Barnes, Derrick. 2020. *I Am Every Good Thing*. Illustrated by Gordon C. James. New York: Nancy Paulsen Books.

Barretta, Gene. 2020. *The Secret Garden of George Washington Carver*. Illustrated by Frank Morrison. New York: Katherine Tegen Books.

Barton, Chris. *Whoosh! Lonnie Johnson's Super-Soaking Stream of Inventions*. Illustrated by Don Tate. Watertown, MA: Charlesbridge.

Beaty, Andrea. 2019. *Sofia Valdez, Future Prez*. Illustrated by David Roberts. New York: Harry N. Abrams.

Browne, Mahogany L., with Elizabeth Acevedo and Olivia Gatwood. 2020. *Woke: A Young Poet's Call to Justice*. Illustrated by Theodore Taylor III. New York: Roaring Brook.

Bryan, Ashley. 2016. *Freedom over Me: Eleven Slaves, Their Lives and Dreams Brought to Life by Ashley Bryan*. New York: Atheneum.

Charles, Tami. 2019. *Fearless Mary: Mary Fields, American Stagecoach Driver*. Illustrated by Claire Almon. Park Ridge, IL: Albert Whitman.

Charles, Tami. 2021. *Freedom Soup*. Illustrated by Jacqueline Alcántara. Somerville, MA: Candlewick.

Clark-Robinson, Monica. 2018. *Let the Children March*. Illustrated by Frank Morrison. New York: Clarion Books.

Cline-Ransome, Lesa. 2020. *The Power of Her Pen: The Story of Groundbreaking Journalist Ethel L. Payne*. Illustrated by John Parra. New York: Simon & Schuster.

Collier, Bryan. 2021. *We Shall Overcome*. New York: Orchard Books.

Cooper, Brittney. 2022. *Stand Up! 10 Mighty Women Who Made a Change*. Illustrated by Cathy Ann Johnson. New York: Orchard Books.

Cortez, Rio. *The ABCs of Black History*. Illustrated by Lauren Semmer. New York: Workman.

Creech, Sharon. 2001. *Love That Dog*. New York: HarperCollins.

Daniele, Kristina Brooke. 2022. *Civil Rights Then and Now: A Timeline of Past and Present Social Justice Issues in America*. Coral Gables, FL: Dragonfruit.

de la Peña, Matt. 2013. *A Nation's Hope: The Story of Boxing Legend Joe Louis*. Illustrated by Kadir Nelson. New York: Puffin Books.

de la Peña, Matt. 2021. *Milo Imagines the World*. Illustrated by Christian Robinson. New York: G. P. Putnam's Sons.

Duncan, Alice Faye. 2022. *Evicted! The Struggle for the Right to Vote*. Illustrated by Charly Palmer. New York: Calkins Creek.

Ellis, Paul. 2014. *The Hero in You*. Illustrated by Angela Padrón. Park Ridge, IL: Albert Whitman.

Ellison, Joy Michael. 2020. *Sylvia and Marsha Start a Revolution! The Story of the Trans Women of Color Who Made LGBTQ+ History*. Illustrated by Teshika Silver. Philadelphia: Jessica Kingsley.

Ewing, Chana Ginelle. 2020. *An ABC of Equality*. Illustrated by Paulina Morgan. London: Frances Lincoln Children's Books.

Giovanni, Nikki. 2007. *Rosa*. Illustrated by Bryan Collier. New York: Square Fish Books.

Hannah-Jones, Nikole, and Renée Watson. 2021. *The 1619 Project: Born on the Water*. Illustrated by Nikkolas Smith. New York: Kokila.

Harrington, Janice N. 2019. *Buzzing with Questions: The Inquisitive Mind of Charles Henry Turner*. Illustrated by Theodore Taylor III. New York: Calkins Creek.

Harrison, Vashti. 2017. *Little Leaders: Bold Women in Black History*. New York: Little, Brown Books for Young Readers.

Harrison, Vashti, with Kwesi Johnson. 2019. *Little Legends: Exceptional Men in Black History*. New York: Little, Brown Books for Young Readers.

Henderson, Leah. 2011. *A Day for Rememberin': Inspired by the True Events of the First Memorial Day*. Illustrated by Floyd Cooper. New York: Harry N. Abrams.

Hill, Laban Carrick. 2013. *When the Beat Was Born: DJ Kool Herc and the Creation of Hip Hop*. Illustrated by Theodore Taylor III. New York: Roaring Brook.

Hillery, Tony. 2020. *Harlem Grown: How One Big Idea Transformed a Neighborhood*. Illustrated by Jessie Hartland. New York: Simon & Schuster.

Hoose, Phillip. 2010. *Claudette Colvin: Twice Toward Justice*. New York: Square Fish Books.

Hudson, Cheryl Willis. 2020. *Brave. Black. First.: 50+ African American Women Who Changed the World*. Illustrated by Erin K. Robinson. New York: Crown Books for Young Readers.

James, Nancy Johnson. 2020. *Brown: The Many Shades of Love*. Illustrated by Constance Moore. New York: Harry N. Abrams.

Johnson, Angela. 2014. *All Different Now: Juneteenth, the First Day of Freedom*. Illustrated by E. B. Lewis. New York: Simon & Schuster Books for Young Readers.

Johnson, Dinah. 2022. *H Is for Harlem*. Illustrated by April Harrison. New York: Christy Ottaviano Books.

Kamkwamba, William, and Bryan Mealer. 2012. *The Boy Who Harnessed the Wind*. Illustrated by Elizabeth Zunon. New York: Dial Books for Young Readers.

King, Shani Mahiri. 2021. *Have I Ever Told You Black Lives Matter*. Illustrated by Bobby C. Martin Jr. Thomaston, ME: Tilbury House.

Kissinger, Kate. 2014. *All the Colors We Are: The Story of How We Get Our Skin Color*. Photographs by Chris Bohnhoff. St. Paul, MN: Redleaf.

Larkin, Shabazz. 2019. *The Thing About Bees: A Love Letter*. San Francisco: Readers to Eaters.

Lewis, Aura, and Evan Sargent. 2020. *We the People: The United States Constitution Explored and Explained*. Beverly, MA: Wide Eyed Editions.

Lord, Michelle. 2020. *Patricia's Vision: The Doctor Who Saved Sight*. Illustrated by Alleanna Harris. New York: Union Square Kids.

Lowe, Mifflin. 2020. *The True West: Real Stories About Black Cowboys, Women Sharpshooters, Native American Rodeo Stars, Pioneering Vaqueros, and the Unsung Explorers, Builders, and Heroes Who Shaped the American West*. Illustrated by William Luong. Charlotte, NC: Baker & Taylor Publisher Services.

Mangal, Mélina. 2018. *The Vast Wonder of the World: Biologist Ernest Everett Just*. Illustrated by Luisa Uribe. Minneapolis: Millbrook.

Marley, Cedella. 2019. *Get Up, Stand Up*. Illustrated by John Jay Cabuay. San Francisco: Chronicle Books.

McLauren, Patrice. 2016. *Have You Thanked an Inventor Today?* Illustrated by Dian Wang. Atlanta: Khemrah.

Medearis, Angela Shelf. 2000. *Seven Spools of Thread: A Kwanzaa Story*. Illustrated by Daniel Minter. Park Ridge, IL: Albert Whitman.

Miller, Sharee. 2018. *Princess Hair*. New York: Little, Brown Books for Young Readers.

Miller, Sharee. 2019. *Don't Touch My Hair*. New York: Little, Brown Books for Young Readers.

Mitchell, Malcolm. 2020. *My Very Favorite Book in the Whole Wide World*. Illustrated by Michael Robertson. New York: Orchard Books.

Myers, Walter Dean. 1997. *Harlem*. Illustrated by Christopher Myers. New York: Scholastic.

Nagara, Innosanto. 2015. *Counting on Community*. New York: Triangle Square.

Nelson, Kadir. 2008. *We Are the Ship: The Story of Negro League Baseball*. New York: Little, Brown Books for Young Readers.

Nelson, Kadir. 2011. *Heart and Soul: The Story of America and African Americans*. New York: Balzer + Bray.

Nelson, Kadir. 2013. *Nelson Mandela*. New York: Katherine Tegen Books.

Nelson, Vaunda Micheaux. 2019. *Let 'Er Buck! George Fletcher, the People's Champion*. Illustrated by Gordon C. James. Minneapolis: Carolrhoda Books.

Newton, Vanessa. 2022. *Let Freedom Sing*. South Orange, NJ: Blue Apple Books.

Norwood, Arlisha. 2020. *Black Heroes: A Black History Book for Kids*. Emeryville, CA: Rockridge.

Paul, Miranda. 2020. *Speak Up*. Illustrated by Ebony Glenn. New York: Clarion Books.

Perkins, Useni Eugene. 2019. *Hey Black Child*. Illustrated by Bryan Collier. New York: LB Kids.

Pinkney, Andrea D. 1999. *Bill Pickett: Rodeo-Ridin' Cowboy*. Illustrated by Brian Pinkney. New York: Clarion Books.

Powell, Patricia Hruby. 2020. *Lift as You Climb: The Story of Ella Baker*. Illustrated by R. Gregory Christie. New York: Margaret K. McElderry Books.

Renaud, Anne. 2017. *Mr. Crum's Potato Predicament*. Illustrated by Felicita Sala. Toronto: Kids Can Press.

Rodaah, Rahma. 2022. *Dear Black Child*. Illustrated by Lydia Mba. New York: Balzer + Bray.

Romito, Dee. 2018. *Pies from Nowhere: How Georgia Gilmore Sustained the Montgomery Bus Boycott*. Illustrated by Laura Freeman. New York: Little Bee Books.

Rose, Tiffany. *M Is for Melanin*. New York: MacMillan Children's Books.

Sanders, Rob. 2018. *Peaceful Fights for Equal Rights*. Illustrated by Jared Andrew Schorr. New York: Simon & Schuster Books for Young Readers.

Sellers, Bakari. 2022. *Who Are Your People?* Illustrated by Reggie Brown. New York: Quill Tree Books.

Shange, Ntozake. 2011. *Coretta Scott*. Illustrated by Kadir Nelson. New York: Katherine Tegen Books.

Smith, Charles R., Jr. 2015. *28 Days: Moments in Black History That Changed the World*. Illustrated by Shane W. Evans. New York: Roaring Brook.

Thompkins-Bigelow, Jamilah. 2022. *Abdul's Story*. Illustrated by Tiffany Rose. New York: Salaam Reads.

Thompkins-Bigelow, Jamilah. 2022. *Hold Them Close: A Love Letter to Black Children*. Illustrated by Patrick Dougher. New York: HarperCollins.

Timelines from Black History: Leaders, Legends and Legacies. 2021. New York: DK.

Velasquez, Eric. 2019. *Octopus Stew*. New York: Holiday House.

Walters, Eric. 2018. *From the Heart of Africa: A Book of Wisdom*. Toronto: Tundra Books.

Weatherford, Carole Boston. 2006. *Moses: When Harriet Tubman Led Her People to Freedom*. Illustrated by Kadir Nelson. New York: Hyperion Books.

Weatherford, Carole Boston. 2009. *The Beatitudes: From Slavery to Civil Rights*. Illustrated by Tim Ladwig. Grand Rapids, MI: Eerdmans Books for Young Readers.

Weatherford, Carole Boston. 2014. *Sugar Hill: Harlem's Historic Neighborhood*. Illustrated by R. Gregory Christie. Park Ridge, IL: Albert Whitman.

Weatherford, Carole Boston. 2019. *The Roots of Rap*: *16 Bars on the 4 Pillars of Hip-Hop*. Illustrated by Frank Morrison. New York: Little Bee Books.

Weatherford, Carole Boston. 2020. *R-E-S-P-E-C-T: Aretha Franklin, the Queen of Soul*. Illustrated by Frank Morrison. New York: Atheneum Books for Young Readers.

Weatherford, Carole Boston. 2021. *Unspeakable: The Tulsa Race Massacre*. Illustrated by Floyd Cooper. Minneapolis: Carolrhoda Books.

Weatherford, Carole Boston, and Rob Sanders. 2022. *A Song for the Unsung: Bayard Rustin, the Man Behind the 1963 March on Washington*. Illustrated by Byron McCray. New York: Henry Holt.

Williams, Schele. 2021. *Your Legacy: A Bold Reclaiming of Our Enslaved History*. Illustrated by Tonya Engle. New York: Harry N. Abrams.

Zoboi, Ibi. 2021. *The People Remember*. Illustrated by Loveis Wise. New York: Balzer + Bray.

Professional References

An, Sohyun. 2020. "First Graders' Inquiry into Multicolored Stories of School (De)Segregation." *Social Studies and the Young Learner* 32 (3): 3–8.

Anderson, Jill. February 23, 2022. "What Is Happening with Critical Race Theory in Education?" HarvardEdCast. https://www.gse.harvard.edu /news/22/02/harvard-edcast-state-critical-race-theory-education.

Au, Wayne, Anthony L. Brown, and Delores Calderón. 2016. *Reclaiming the Multicultural Roots of U.S. Curriculum: Communities of Color and Official Knowledge in Education*. Multicultural Education Series, ed. James A. Banks. New York: Teachers College Press.

Barnes, Derrick. August 16, 2022. "Instagram Live with Dawnavyn James." Instagram. https://www.instagram.com/tv/ChVsX7bBBJ9/?utm_source =ig_web_copy_link.

Bennett, Brad. 2020. "Honoring Emmett Till: 65 Years After Brutal Murder That Galvanized Civil Rights Movement, Family Still Seeking Justice." Southern Poverty Law Center. https://www.splcenter.org/news/2020/08/28 /honoring-emmett-till-65-years-after-brutal-murder-galvanized-civil -rights-movement-family.

Bird, Betsy. January 5, 2021. "An Unspeakable Interview: Talking with Carole Boston Weatherford and Floyd Cooper About the Tulsa Race Massacre." *School Library Journal*. https://afuse8production.slj.com/2021/01/05 /an-unspeakable-interview-talking-with-carole-boston-weatherford-about -the-tulsa-race-massacre/.

Bishop, Rudine Sims. 1990. "Mirrors, Windows, and Sliding Glass Doors." *Perspectives: Choosing and Using Books for the Classroom* 6 (3): ix–xi.

Bundles, A'Lelia. 2002. *On Her Own Ground: The Life and Times of Madam C. J. Walker*. New York: Scribner.

Eckart, Kim. 2017. "Promoting self-esteem among African-American girls through racial, cultural connections." *UW News*. December 21. https: //www.washington.edu/news/2017/12/21/promoting-self-esteem-among -african-american-girls-through-racial-cultural-connections/.

Emmett, Jennifer. 2012. "Explore Your World: Crafting Today's Nonfiction for Kids." Society of Children's Book Writers and Illustrators Eastern Upstate Chapter's Falling Leaves Masterclass Writing Retreat, Silver Bay, New York.

Garrow, David J. 2015. *Bearing the Cross: Martin Luther King, Jr., and the Southern Christian Leadership Conference*. New York: Open Road Media.

Givens, Jarvis R. 2021. *Fugitive Pedagogy: Carter G. Woodson and the Art of Black Teaching*. Cambridge, MA: Harvard University Press.

Glazé, Leo (@IAmLeoGlaze). 2021. "When Students ask teachers not to sugarcoat history, they're asking their teachers not to lie to them. There are age appropriate ways to tell the truth without lying." Twitter, December 8, 2021, 2:21 p.m. https://twitter.com/iamleoglaze/status /1468662110494199813?lang=ar.

Johnson, Aeriale. 2021. "An Educator's Guide to *The 1619 Project: Born on the Water*." New York: Penguin Books. https://storage.googleapis.com /classroom-portal-production/uploads/2021/11/512a7c15-bornonthewater _edguide.pdf.

Johnson, Wintre Foxworth. 2022. "History Is a Way of Building Identity: How One Independent Neighborhood Elementary School Uses Black Cultural Movements to Engage Children's Sociopolitical Perspectives." *Language Arts* 99 (3): 167–78.

Love, David A. February 28, 2022. "What's Really Lost When Schools Only Make Black History Month Lessons Optional." *NBC News*. https://www.nbcnews .com/think/opinion/black-history-month-dealt-us-painful-reminder -ncna1290130.

Mills Quarterly. March 30, 2022. "SOE Centers Antiracism in Teacher Education." https://quarterly.mills.edu/soe-centers-antiracism-in -teacher-education/.

Missouri Department of Elementary and Secondary Education. 2016. "K–5 Social Studies Grade Level Expectations." https://dese.mo.gov/media/pdf /curr-mls-standards-ss-k-5-sboe-2016.

Nodjimbadem, Katie. February 13, 2017. "The Lesser-Known History of African-American Cowboys." *Smithsonian Magazine*. https://www .smithsonianmag.com/history/lesser-known-history-african-american -cowboys-180962144/.

Origins of Everything. 2018. "Is the Rosa Parks Story True?" PBS Digital Studios. https://www.pbs.org/video/is-the-rosa-parks-story-true-zw9irm/.

Parks, Rosa, with Jim Haskins. 1992. *Rosa Parks: My Story*. New York: Puffin Books.

Patterson, Timothy J., and Jay M. Shuttleworth. 2020. "Teaching Hard History Through Children's Literature About Enslavement." *Social Studies and the Young Learner* 32 (3): 14–19.

Pitts, Brianne. 2020. "Black History Month in Suburban Schools: An Examination of K–12 Pedagogies." PhD diss., University of Wisconsin–Madison.

Rodríguez, Noreen Naseem, Anna Falkner, and Elizabeth Tetu Bohl. 2022. "Reading Beyond the Book with Primary Sources." *Reading Teacher* 75 (6): 749–54.

Rodríguez, Noreen Naseem, and Katy Swalwell. 2022. *Social Studies for a Better World: An Anti-Oppressive Approach for Elementary Educators*. New York: W. W. Norton.

Sealey-Ruiz, Yolanda. February 12, 2022. "Historical Literacy as Racial Literacy." Black History Nerds Saturday School, University at Buffalo Center for K–12 Black History and Racial Literacy Education. Presentation via Zoom.

Stewart, Melissa, and Marlene Correia. 2021. *5 Kinds of Nonfiction: Enriching Reading and Writing Instruction with Children's Books*. Portsmouth, NH: Stenhouse.

Taylor, Nicole A. 2022. *Watermelon and Red Birds: A Cookbook for Juneteenth and Black Celebrations*. New York: Simon & Schuster.

Theoharis, Jeanne. 2021. *The Rebellious Life of Mrs. Rosa Parks (Adapted for Young People)*. Adapted by Brandy Colbert and Jeanne Theoharis. Boston: Beacon Press.

Tipton-Martin, Toni. 2019. *Jubilee: Recipes from Two Centuries of African American Cooking*. New York: Clarkson Potter.

Tulino, Daniel P., Greg Simmons, and Brianne R. Pitts. February 16, 2021. "How Can White Teachers Teach Black History? Six Thing You Need to Know." https://www.edweek.org/teaching-learning/opinion-how-can-white-teachers-teach-black-history-six-things-you-need-to-know/2021/02.

Vella, Christina. 2015. *George Washington Carver: A Life*. Baton Rouge: Louisiana State University Press.

Vickery, Amanda. July 2018. "Reclaiming Our Time: Using Journey Boxes to Teach Black Women's History." Session presented at the Teaching Black History Conference, Carter Center for K–12 Black History Education.

Wellington, Paul A. 2019. *Black Built: History and Architecture in the Black Community*. Self-published.

White, April. May 4, 2017. "The Story of the Invention of the Potato Chip Is a Myth." *JStor Daily*. https://daily.jstor.org/story-invention-potato-chip-myth/.

Wolfe-Rocca, Ursula, and Christie Nold. August 2, 2022. "Why the Narrative That Critical Race Theory 'Makes White Kids Feel Guilty' Is a Lie." *Hechinger Report*. https://hechingerreport.org/opinion-why-the-narrative-that-critical-race-theory-makes-white-kids-feel-guilty-is-a-lie/.

Yorio, Kara. October 23, 2018. "#OwnVoices Not Familiar to All." *School Library Journal*. https://www.slj.com/story/ownvoices-not-familiar-all.

Index

D

E

F

G

H

I

J

P

Q

Credits

Chapter 1

Figure 1.2, © AP Photo / Bill Ingraham.

Figure 1.3, OUT OF WONDER. Text copyright © 2017 by Kwame Alexander. Illustrations copyright © 2017 by Ekua Holmes. Reproduced by permission of the publisher, Candlewick Press, Somerville, MA.

Figure 1.5, Cover from HARLEM by Walter Dean Myers, illustrated by Christopher Myers. Cover art copyright © 1997 by Christopher Myers. Reprinted by permission of Scholastic Inc.

Cover of *Civil Rights Then & Now: A Timeline of Past and Present Social Justice Issues in America* by Kristina Brooke Daniele. Illustrated by Lindsey Bailey. © 2022 Dragonfruit Publishing. Used by permission of the publisher.

Photo of Rosa Parks, © AP Photo/Gene Herrick.

Cover of *The Rebellious Life of Mrs. Rosa Parks (Adapted for Young People)* by Jeanne Theoharis. Adapted by Brandy Colbert and Jeanne Theoharis. © 2021 Beacon Press. Used by permission from the publisher.

Photo of Harriet Tubman, © National Archives Catalog.

From *Moses* by Carole Boston Weatherford, copyright © 2006. Reprinted by permission of LBYR Plus, an imprint of Hachette Book Group, Inc.

Photo of George Washington Carver, © National Parks Service Gallery.

Photo of Martin Luther King Jr., © Bettmann / Getty Images.

WHAT COLOR IS MY WORLD? Text copyright © 2012 by Kareem Abdul-Jabbar and Raymond Obstfeld. Illustrations copyright © 2012 by Ben Boos and A. G. Ford. Reproduced by permission of the publisher, Candlewick Press, Somerville, MA.

Cover and interior from *Have You Thanked an Inventor Today?* by Patrice McLaurin. Illustrated by Dian Wang. © 2016 Khemrah Publishing. Used with permission from the publisher.

Photo of Ella Baker, © AP Photo/Jack Harris.

Photo of Georgia Gilmore, © Alabama Department of Archives and History.

Cover of *Fearless Mary*. Text copyright © 2019 by Tami Charles. Illustration copyright © 2019 by Albert Whitman & Co. Illustrations by Claire Almon. Published by Albert Whitman & Co. All rights reserved.

Cover only from *Who Are Your People?* by Bakari Sellers. Illustrated by Reggie Brown. Read by Bakari Sellers. Cover copyright © 2022 by Reggie Brown. Used by permission of HarperCollins Publishers.

From YOUR LEGACY, written by Schele Williams and illustrated by Tonya Engel. Text and illustrations copyright © 2021 Schele Williams. Used by permission of Abrams Books for Young Readers, an imprint of ABRAMS, New York. All rights reserved.

Chapter 2

Interior only from *Let the Children March* by Monica Clark Robinson. Illustrated by Frank Morrison. Text copyright © 2018 by Monica Clark Robinson. Art copyright © 2018 by Frank Morrison. Used by permission of HarperCollins Publishers.

Text © 2019 Atinuke. Illustrations © 2019 Mouni Feddag. From AFRICA, AMAZING AFRICA: COUNTRY BY COUNTRY Written by Atinuke & Illustrated by Mouni Feddag. Reproduced by permission of Walker Books Ltd, London, SE11 5HJ www.walker.co.uk.

Cover only from *Nelson Mandela* by Kadir Nelson. Illustrated by Kadir Nelson. Copyright (c) 2013 by Kadir Nelson. Used by permission of HarperCollins Publishers.

Cover of *The 1619 Project: Born on the Water* by Nikole Hannah-Jones and Renée Watson. Illustrated by Nikkolas Smith. © 2021 Penguin Random House.

Cover of *From the Heart of Africa: A Book of Wisdom* by Eric Walters. © 2018 Tundra Books. Used with permission of the publisher.